Lutheran Questions
Lutheran Answers

D0395757

Lutheran Questions
Lutheran Answers

Exploring Christian Faith

Martin E. Marty

Augsburg Books

MINNEAPOLIS

LUTHERAN QUESTIONS, LUTHERAN ANSWERS
Exploring Christian Faith

Library of Congress Cataloging-in-Publication Data
Marty, Martin E., 1928-
  Lutheran questions, Lutheran answers : exploring Christian faith / Martin E. Marty.
    p. cm.
  Includes bibliographical references and index.
  ISBN-13: 978-0-8066-5350-1 (alk. paper)
  ISBN-10: 0-8066-5350-7 (alk. paper)
  1. Lutheran Church—Doctrines—Miscellanea. 2. Lutheran Church—Miscellanea. 3. Theology—Miscellanea. I. Title.
  BX8065.3.M37 2007
  284.1—dc22   2007007992

Cover design by Dave Meyer; cover photo © Stockdisc Premium/Getty Images. Used by permission.

Book design by Michelle L. N. Cook and Christy J. P. Barker

Manufactured in the U.S.A.

Contents

Invitation

Christian faith has to do less with what you know and more with whom you know, namely, God and God in Christ. Yet the "what" of Christian knowledge also matters greatly, because all kinds of stories, events, memories, doctrines, and programs enrich the faith. In faith as in the rest of life, a person grows in knowledge by asking questions.

Christian leaders, therefore, welcome questions of all sorts, and Lutherans especially like to say that they do. The Small Catechism, through which so many children as well as adults learn about Lutheran expressions of the faith, is made up of questions and answers: "What does this mean?" appears scores of times.

Some questions have to deal simply with information. What does the Bible say? What has the church taught? What is expected of me? Others have a skeptical tinge to them. Lutherans encourage critical inquiry. These questions might deal with the faith and science, or with the very nature of God. Rather than suppress such questions, Lutherans encourage inquiry, discussion, and research.

The Presbyterians, who have the same interests as Lutherans, published a little book by Donald K. McKim that we found to be a model of empathy and anticipation. The author put himself in the role of the non-believer, non-Christian, or non-Presbyterian and anticipated what such a person might ask. This book draws on that model, and its author and publisher hope other Christian communions will pick up and trade on the example until there is a little shelf of question and answer books.

I am sometimes asked how I happen to be a Lutheran Christian. The answer: because of linguistic confusion. In Switzerland, "Evangelicals" are "Reformed," not Lutheran. When my great-grandparents migrated to Nebraska, possessing no Yellow Pages that listed churches by denominations, they must have asked for the nearest "evangelische Kirche [church]" and were sent to the

Lutheran parish down the road. I have had almost eight decades to question this, in my view, happy accidental choice and the heritage that nurtured me. I remain Lutheran.

Lutheran accents on the Christian story and creeds are not the whole of the Christian witness. Other communions and confessions bring their own emphases and particular views. Just as in the rest of life, however, we need a place to stand to view the world. So in Christian faith we bring the strengths of our particular witness, experience, location, and inventiveness, offering it to others in exchange for what they bring and offer.

So now it is in place for me to invite you into an imagined conversation, where we hope you will picture yourself probing, as individuals long have done, or discussing, as groups have done and will do. No one can speak authoritatively for all Lutheran groups and interests, but I have tried to be representative of those who deal with main themes. No one can give final or always satisfying partial answers. Those in this Q and A book are not last words, but first words, directed at people some of whom will also come up with their own answers, having used these as a guide.

We, author and publisher, offer this book as a resource both for individuals and for group study. Individuals will find it useful as they prepare for membership in a Lutheran congregation, or as a refresher on what they learned years ago, or perhaps as a student or seeker looking for a convenient introduction to Lutheranism. The thirteen chapters also are suitable for adult group study over a period of one quarter of the church year. The question and answer format functions as a stimulus for discussion. Portions of the book also lend themselves for use in church council meetings, new members classes, and retreats.

I have tried to speak with an inviting tone, one that beckons the reader to make her or his own contribution. I welcome what I hear by way of response, since this will help me and leaders in the church better address the curiosities, needs, and interests of old-timers and newcomers alike. We have much to learn *together*.

—Martin E. Marty

chapter one

Lutheran History and Heritage

1. Where Do Lutheran Churches Come From?

The Lutheran movement, from which Lutheran churches
have come, began in a small area of Europe almost five
centuries ago. A map of its extent as of 1600 shows how
small that territory was. All of Scandinavia had become Lutheran,
most of the regions that make up today's Germany and some of
the Baltic nations were mainly Lutheran, and there were Lutheran
cities—virtual islands—in areas Lutherans shared with Catholics
and Calvinists, especially in Central Europe. From this sliver of
bases on the map of northern Europe, Lutherans have gone on to
become a worldwide movement of almost seventy million people, and their churches and members are well represented on five
continents.

"Where are Lutheran churches going?" is a question that
evokes answers guaranteed to startle many who think of the movement as being northern European and North American. Early
in this new millennium there are more Lutherans in Africa and
there will soon be more in Asia than in North America. Europe
still has more Lutherans on the books, but the fresh activity is in
the non-European world. While North American Lutheranism
declined by 4 percent in the ten years surrounding the turn of
this century to just more than eight million, the African Lutheran

churches grew by 63 percent to more than fourteen million, while Asia numbers more than seven million Lutherans.

Where have they come from? The Reformation has been described by a university-minded scholar as "a revolt of the junior faculty at Wittenberg University" in Saxony, because there a fervent monk, the biblical scholar Martin Luther, in conscience opposed many of the dominant Roman Catholic teachings and practices. With their books and ideas spreading, thanks to the recent invention of printing, he and his university colleagues soon found company far beyond their original bases, just as they increasingly antagonized the Catholic leaders. These reformers were eager to participate in a church council where their teachings would have gotten a hearing, but they found that their efforts to promote one were utterly futile. Nonetheless, with the backing of German-speaking princes, who resented Rome's spiritual rule, and with growing numbers of ordinary believers who welcomed the biblical teachings of God's free grace, the movement quickly spread. After a decade or two of protest they found themselves moving out and being moved out of their Roman connection and founding churches of their own.

The name "Lutheran" was not one that Luther liked or that Lutherans chose; it was pinned on them. They found allies in protest and reform among Christians in Switzerland, the Netherlands, Scotland, and central Europe—Calvinists, Zwinglians, Presbyterians, and more—though differences over numerous teachings kept them from becoming more than a part of a loosely connected group that came to be called "Protestant" or "Evangelical."

In the eighteenth century Lutherans spread to North America, and in the nineteenth into much of the world, so that in and after the twentieth century their more than eighty thousand congregations can be found in some two hundred Lutheran denominations at home in more than one hundred nations. This highly varied and sometimes contentious cluster of church bodies is united by an approach to the Christian gospel focused on the Lutheran "Confessions," statements of belief drafted in the sixteenth century and holding sway ever since.

2. What Are the Origins of Lutheran Churches in the United States?

Lutheran churches in America originated when European immigrants arrived and began preaching and gathering as congregations. You can find the name "Lutheran" as early as 1564 in Florida, but that was a case of mistaken identity: Spanish Catholics on the scene called all Protestants "Lutheran." In colonial times Lutherans and most other Christian groups were unwelcome in New England, where Congregationalist churches were established by law and supported by taxes, and in southern colonies, where the Anglican or Episcopal church was official.

Like so many other later-comers, therefore, the earliest Lutherans found themselves at home after 1638 in Pennsylvania, Delaware, and New Jersey, the middle colonies where religious freedom prevailed. Most of them spoke Swedish or, more regularly, German in colonies where English was dominant. So they had a hard time making an impact in the larger culture, and some chose to keep to themselves, speaking their own languages. A century ago one Lutheran observed that every week the gospel was being preached in eighteen different languages in Lutheran pulpits. Today almost everywhere in North America only English is spoken, though new congregations are often Spanish-speaking.

Lutherans came in larger numbers in the eighteenth century, organizing with the first ordination of a pastor in 1703 and the first connection of congregations, the Ministerium of Pennsylvania, in 1748. In the nineteenth century, often because of bad economic times in Europe and good economic prospects in the United States, but also sometimes to protest official Lutheranism in Germany and Scandinavia, Lutherans came in large numbers. By the nineteenth century many had moved west to states surrounding the Great Lakes, some to southern states, and many to the upper Midwest, though their steeples show up on horizons of town and country "from sea to shining sea."

Coming as they did from so many nations with so many languages, traditions, customs, and theological accents, they were often strangers to each other. Not until the late nineteenth century did many of them join together in large merged denominations or federations. Today more than five million are in the Evangelical Lutheran Church in America, half that many in the Lutheran Church—Missouri Synod, and several hundred thousand in small bodies.

Church governance varies among Lutherans, who seldom have defined precisely or prescribed exactly what polity, what arrangement, should prevail. Everywhere congregations have considerable degrees of freedom to set their policies, but most are responsive to synods and the action of national assemblies and conventions. Clergy are ordained and congregations registered in relation to those Lutheran confessions that date back to the origins five centuries ago.

3. What Do We Mean by a "Lutheran" Church or "Lutheran" Theology?

E very Lutheran congregation or church body in the world will tell you that their church and theology are first of all Christian in the inclusive sense of being responsive most of all to the sacred Scriptures focused in the gospel of Jesus Christ and in worship of the Holy Trinity. Lutherans first called themselves evangelical, because they preached the "evangel," or "gospel." Many present-day "evangelicals" and other Protestants join with Lutherans in professing creeds that identify them with the "one, holy, *catholic*, and apostolic" church. Each large bloc or cluster of churches, such as the Anglican/Episcopal, Presbyterian, Methodist, and more, however, will insist on certain interpretations of the Bible and stress special aspects of the faith, and Lutherans are usually listed as being more specific about these than many bodies.

As for Lutheran theology, Lutherans have sometimes encountered beliefs and accusations that they worshiped or at least overly revered Martin Luther. This has never been the case. Luther defined his theology as he went along, sometimes correcting himself and often letting apparently contradictory assertions stand unexplained. Until he died in 1546, he argued with fellow Wittenberg theologians and others who signed the Lutheran Confessions, which were written between 1530 and 1580. Lutherans who suffered under oppression in Catholic-dominated lands or under authoritarian rule came up with different theological accents than did those "born free," where freedom and prosperity abounded. Still, through it all, Lutheran theology involves some consistencies that separate it from Catholicism, Eastern Orthodoxy, and most other Protestantism. Their historic Confessions are designed less to say, "This you must believe!" and more to indicate, "This is what we believe, this is who we are, this is your key to understanding us."

The main Lutheran accents involve attempts to be faithful to the Scriptures, accepting their full authority and drawing from them the central theme that God is a God of judgment *and* mercy who relates to humans through Jesus Christ and by the power of the Holy Spirit, and that nothing in that relation is more important than "faith" and "grace." Everything else flows from these themes. Lutheran theology is the interpretation of reality in the light of these commitments.

4. What Is Lutheranism?

Lutheranism is a whole complex of witness, gathering, practice, and cultural impact. One must make some distinctions among these. Thus Lutheran culture can remain strong, at least for a time, where Lutheran practice is weak. Here one thinks of the empty pews and bare altars in many churches of Europe, and not Europe alone. Still, mapmakers will list the place where Lutheran churches were once strong as Lutheran and the culture as one where the long shadow of Lutheranism is still present. In this sense, Lutheranism can have an influence, often unrecognized, in the arts—especially music—and politics and style or custom. Many observers claim that social welfare programs in nations like Sweden, where church participation is very low, reveal the long-term influence of the Lutheran presence, which means that Lutheranism is there in some vague form.

Lutheranism takes life, however, where people actively participate, attending worship and regularly experiencing the sacraments, preaching, teaching, and counseling in line with the gospel and the Lutheran Confessions. In some bodies the teaching is closely supervised, and most argument—argument does find a home in Lutheranism!—has to do with who deviates from this or that interpretation of the creeds and Confessions. For example, some American Lutheran churches contend that their leaders and, implicitly, all members must vow faithfulness to the Confessions *quia*, "because" they are perfectly congruent with the Scriptures, and others say they would be faithful *quatenus*, "to the degree that" they are faithful to the biblical texts. Not many in the congregations know those Latin words and most might not care, but they do point to some tests that some Lutherans would make and to some liberties others would say the gospel permits them to take. Anyone from a church body a few inches away from Lutheranism might wonder what such arguments are about, since at least some of the Confessions—the two catechisms of Martin Luther and the Augsburg Confession of 1530—have such a cherished place.

Beyond this, Lutheranism shows up in practices such as singing hymns; showing regard for the pastoral office; teaching the Bible, the catechism, and other sources to the young; and asking members to make their "faith active in love" (see Galatians 5:6).

5. Why Do Lutherans Have So Many Confessions of Faith?

They don't have "so many"; it often only seems that way. They are collected in a seven- or eight-hundred-page volume, *The Book of Concord*, whose bulk suggests many. The actual count is three plus seven. The three, part of the official collection, are the "three ecumenical creeds," shared with Catholics, Eastern Orthodox, and most "orthodox" Protestant bodies. (Some of the latter may be very serious about theology but resist the idea of invoking "human-made creeds.")

Lutherans take their Confessions with varying degrees of seriousness and devotion. The Small Catechism has often been the "mother's milk" of Lutheran nurture, taught by catechists on mountainsides in Papua New Guinea, in secret anti-Nazi seminaries, and in suburban parishes alike. The Large Catechism is a gem, based on sermons by Luther when he was defining what he taught in a crucial moment as Lutheranism was being formed. The Augsburg Confession is decisive for defining and witnessing. By the way, the superscript to its Latin version, a verse Luther favored from Psalm 119:46, suggests why Lutherans have so many Confessions: *they enjoy them.* That verse reflects the fact that the Lutheran party, standing down "the Invincible Emperor, Charles V, Caesar Augustus, in the City of Augsburg," reads, "I will also speak of your decrees before kings, and shall not be put to shame." They like the boldness, almost the bravado, the zest for witnessing to the gospel in the Confessions at their best.

Admittedly, not all pages of all confessions speak to everyone all the time. They reflect controversies that took place between 1529 and 1577 within Lutheranism, among Protestants, and with Catholics. Also admittedly, most pastors do not look up something in the confessional document Treatise on the Power and Primacy of the Pope (1537) before making sick calls or writing sermons. Most would confess about the Confessions that dust is thick on some of them—some have been untouched since seminary days and were lightly treated then. If it is true that nothing is more useless than an answer to an unasked question, one must say that some pages reflect "old, unhappy, far-off things, and battles long ago."

Amazingly, however, the heart and core of the confessions do address many of the great issues of the ages, including our own. A serious pastor or other informed members may critique their emphases and some of their points, but most of them show respect and find reason to consult them when defining the Lutheran witness to the gospel and the life of the church.

6. What Makes Lutherans Different from Presbyterians or Methodists or Baptists?

T he way that question is put makes answering somewhat difficult. If we are asked what makes Lutherans different from Buddhists or Hindus, Muslims or Jews, it would be easy to reach for the center and make faith in the Holy Trinity and belief in the saving work of Jesus Christ the definers. For most Lutherans it may also not be so difficult to say what makes Lutherans different from Roman Catholics. In the main, the war is over, in the sense that there was a total breach between these two sets of Christians who had had trouble laying down their arms and extending their greeting hands decades ago. But so much has happened during recent decades in many areas of difference that they can both speak of common affirmations. And yet no one can fail to spot the differences when they count the number of sacraments or point to the authority of the pope within Roman Catholicism..

With Protestant kin the answer does grow more difficult, because Presbyterians, Methodists, Baptists—and add Mennonites, Episcopalians, Disciples of Christ, and so many more—have so much in common with Lutherans. We are all Christians, in many ways Protestants, ordinarily claiming the full authority of the Scriptures, being devoted to the grace of God in Christ, celebrating the sacraments. (Some Lutheran critics of these bodies often suggest that Lutherans should have nothing to do with others because some are too "liberal" or others too "conservative," some too "literalist," others too "free in interpretation." Such concerns are in place, but they do not determine everything, and they may inspire both some measures of Christian charity toward these others and the use of the mirror by Lutherans on themselves as they repent and revise and change.)

Many Lutherans are in "full communion" with numbers of the bodies and movements mentioned in the question, but they do not deny that differences exist. G. Elson Ruff, a Lutheran editor, once was asked whether Lutherans believe that theirs is the only true faith; he answered, "Yes, they just don't believe that they alone hold it." The differing emphases among them remain important, and for those Lutheran bodies who favor high walls, thick boundaries, and distance from others (these are not insulting terms but descriptions they would welcome), they are so great that such Lutherans cannot have fellowship with them or, in some cases, even appreciate their witness and work.

To be sure, there are distinctions, some of them having to do with emphases. To illustrate: Followers of John Calvin ("Reformed" Protestants) begin with witness to the sovereign God and relate God's graciousness to it. Lutherans begin with God's grace and have to work out what this means for God's sovereignty. The former wrestle with some version or other of "predestination," how one can be sure of grace if God "foreknows" and "predestines" salvation or damnation. The latter wrestle with "cheap grace," which means that people can so accent God's grace that they turn casual and careless, not giving enough accent to the seriousness of God's claim, call, and judgment.

Differences show up in the understandings of what goes on in baptism and the Lord's Supper, in interpreting the depth and extent of human sin and what humans and God do about it, and in numberless practices. The differences are or seem great enough to keep the churches from merging into one and losing positive accents, and small enough to promote common Christian witness and celebration.

7. Do Lutherans Believe in "Predestination"?

P redestination is a very serious, even urgent doctrine. Various answers to questions about predestination have tortured many souls, thrown them into terror of uncertainty, or led to a shrug of apathy over mysteries that cannot be completely penetrated.

The problem comes up once one has witnessed to the all-powerful, all-knowing, everywhere-present sovereign God. If God is really in control—and if not in control, can God really be God?—then God is witnessed to as being in control of past, present, and future, creating and determining the destiny of all humans. Where does human will, decision, or response come in? Luther and the Lutherans, when serious, had to deal with such questions as much as Presbyterians and the Reformed ever did.

Looking over the fence that separated Luther from Calvin and the traditions that they helped advance, it is easy to be flip about the differences. Wags misstate the Calvinist teaching by cracking jokes such as the one about the Presbyterian woman who, at age eighty-four, fell down the steps and shattered her hip, only to moan in praise: "Well, thank God, *that* one is over." And a Presbyterian can quote a Lutheran bishop who looked at fellow Lutherans who were blithe about the sovereignty of God and observed that "there is nothing so slack as a slack Lutheran."

This question has roots in the earliest moments of Lutheranism, when Luther, his soul figuratively twisting and turning as his body writhed on the monastery cell floor, asked how he could know whether God was gracious and whether God's grace extended to him. "How can I know if I am among the elect, those predestined to be saved?" While his confessor, Johannes Staupitz, weary of hearing the question from the overly scrupulous monk, did not settle everything, he did point in the right direction. To condense and paraphrase it, he said something like this: "Martin, you are trying to peer into the divine majesty, as if you were God and could know the mind of God. You are not God and cannot resolve everything about the nature of God. You are starting at the wrong end of the sequence of questions. You are beginning with the unknown. Instead, start with the known, which means the wounds of a suffering Christ, the knowledge of God's act of love. Let the rest flow from there." Elaborating on that kind of witness has led Lutherans still to care about the providence of God and even about predestination.

chapter two

The Bible

8. What Is the Basic Message of the Bible?

Many scholars have tried to boil down the thesis of the sixty-six books of the Bible into one simple and coherent plot and give it a label. The most favored among some in the century past was "the history of salvation." Many scholars and general readers of the Bible, however, criticized the attempt and the result. In effect, they said that all its writings can't be fit into a single basic category. The Bible is not a book but a library. Most readers would have a hard time fitting the book of Ecclesiastes or Song of Songs into a pattern of salvation history. Any attempt to speak of the basic message has to come with the tags "Handle with Care" and "Watch for the Limits."

Having said all those cautionary words, I come back to the question and say that the attempt to find coherence in the Bible is not foolish but well intentioned, and answers to it will help readers find their way through its complexities. Philosopher Eugen Rosenstock-Huessy said, "One book is about one thing; at least the good ones are." The Gospel of Mark is about one thing, as is Paul's letter to the Romans. But bind them all between two covers and look for the basic thread? That is more difficult.

In this book of Lutheran questions and answers, it is better to pose the question somewhat differently: What do Lutherans

take from the Bible and call basic? There is no doubt that almost
five centuries of study, practice, and custom lead them to bring
certain curiosities and quests to the Bible and to find responses to
these. Here are some of the main themes:

• *God is the main character, but this God interacts with
humans.* Whoever reads the Bible and thinks it is about David or
Isaiah or Peter will be thrown off. The book is creatively, almost
fiercely devoted to God the Creator, the God of Israel, God the
one whom Jesus calls "Abba" (Father). Now and then whispers
of talk about God among the gods show up, but they get cut off
quickly. No Muslim for whom Allah is One and All would be
more devoted to one God than are Christians.

• *God who interacts with humans does so out of love.* The Bible
is a book in which, whatever else happens, witness to the love
of God or to God as love is basic. On many pages the theme is
emphatically stated: "God is love. . . ." Note that it does not say
that "love is God." The Bible in its basic message says that, however much we are confronted by a God of power and might, a
God of judgment and justice, we have not gotten to the basis until
we come to see God's motion toward us in the form of love. And
since love is the mark and love reaches out, the Bible constantly
shows God seeking and grasping and holding us.

• *In the created order, things are not as they ought to be.* That
is, God intends a perfect and complete created order, but ours
is imperfect and broken, and at the heart of that creation is the
human who by participating in the human race occupies a world
in which things are not as they ought to be. They should be holy,
but we are unholy. What is more, while we "ought" to right that
broken world, while we can do some repair jobs, we cannot "fix"
the whole situation. We are not as we ought to be. All of us. All
the way down deep.

• *God, being a God of love, cannot abandon the created world or us humans within it.* The whole creation, writes Paul in Romans 8, "groans" and "is in travail" and "awaits" redemption, to be bought back by God and brought back to God. And God takes action that invites our welcome and response.

• *The agent of that "righting" of things to what they ought to be is God, now in Jesus Christ.* God's work is begun and further anticipated in the Old Testament in the story of God's dealings with a people, Israel. That work advances through the words of God's prophets. But the climax, the decisive act that changes everything, is God's saving and healing and restoring action in the man Christ Jesus, who is also the exalted Lord (Philippians 2:5–11).

• *In Jesus Christ we participate in the new creation.* Evil in the old creation caused God in Christ to suffer through Jesus' death, but the basic message of the Bible shows that that is not the last word. God vindicated Jesus by raising him from the dead and makes the gift of Jesus our own: we are, with him, the "first fruits of the new creation," and from now on nothing will separate us from the love of God.

• *Through the Holy Spirit God intends and effects community in which we praise God and serve others.* We call this community "the church" or "the Body of Christ."

• *The earth and the history we know are not the last word.* The basic message of the Bible says that history has a beginning and an end, but the purposes of the eternal and loving God are not exhausted by the end of history, so the end of the basic message is this: we live.

9. What Is the Purpose of the Bible?

Lutherans might begin to answer this question by saying something about what the purpose of the Bible is not. For example, it is not a textbook on science, a reference work to which we pose questions and get answers about the natural world. It speaks a great deal about that natural world, but its goal is to have us relate that world to God, not to the physics classroom.

Next, it is not a book of rules, a log of hundreds of "do this's" and "don't do that's," although one can read in it and deduce from it many bits of good advice about how to live and think. Thinking of it as a rulebook leads to forgetting what its basic message is. That message is not "Follow these rules and all will be well. Comply with enough of them and a holy God will be satisfied. Learn them and you can judge your neighbor who is not quite up to your standards and can't match your achievements."

The Bible, furthermore, is not a guide to success. You will hear from some promoters that you will benefit financially if you practice stewardship as the Bible urges, or that the parables are good lessons in successful management. The fact that the Bible says we have to lose in order to win and die in order to live makes clear that God turns the world topsy-turvy. Very often those who can't know worldly success are most vividly portrayed as the children of God.

The Bible lets us know that God is in control and that we should consult it in all circumstances involving doubt and faith. When we are on our high horses, the Bible, through many stories and sayings, helps knock us down. More important, since we are often to be in the shadows and sloughs, to walk in the valley of decision and be threatened at the chasm of despair, the Bible witnesses to the fact that a loving God remains in control and that our lives and years are in God's hand.

All this becomes most clear in the words and works of Jesus Christ. The New Testament is most clear about how the God who is in control leaves power behind (again, Philippians 2) and reaches down to our level, becoming one of us and one with us. He shouted, "My God, my God, why have you forsaken me?" but he is the last one ever to have reason to feel abandoned by God, and after his resurrection no one need ever again be alone. The purpose of the Bible is to show us the company of God and help us realize it.

There are other purposes of the Bible that go with these. They help us find our identity, our place, our vocation, our freedom, our relations to others. But all the purposes are wrapped up in what is unfolded with the gift of Christ.

10. What Do We Mean When We Say the Bible Is "God's Word"?

Lutherans yield to no others when it comes to celebrating the Word, God's Word, Christ as the Word of God, and, along with all these, the Bible as God's Word.

Ever since the beginning of Lutheranism, Lutherans have stood in awe of the fact that everything begins with the Word of God and that, while the mountains and worlds may cease, the Word of the Lord endures forever. There may be hundreds of thousands of billions of galaxies, each of them loaded with hundreds of thousands of billions of stars, but as far as humans are concerned, everything is chaotic and meaningless—and silent?—until, as in Genesis 1, God speaks, God says something. That is a startling thought that deserves reflection.

Just as the activity of God throughout the Bible is identified with breaking silence—with speaking—with the Word, so the clearest address to each of us and all of us arrives when beyond the chaos and creation of nature Jesus appears as the Word, the *logos*, which is an interesting way of speaking about a human: Jesus does not just speak words. He *is* the Word, the connecting link with God. That ought to be enough.

We believe, however, that God gives us more. And that "more" is written on scrolls or printed in books. Hollywood producer Sam Goldwyn, known for malapropisms and boners, once snorted, "An oral agreement isn't worth the paper it's printed on." He mangled his concepts, but we know what he was getting at. In our context, an "oral agreement" between God and Abraham or Noah or Israel or the disciples could have been forgotten or passed along inaccurately. The Bible is a kind of written agreement or, in its own terms, a "covenant." That form makes us more sure of how God acts and what God says.

Martin Luther sometimes seems to give the printed word in the Bible secondary status. He liked "the living word" and said in a German pun that the Word of God is more to be "shouted" than "written" (*geschrien*, not *geschrieben*). But the spoken, living, shouted word for Luther *always* derives from and relates to the Word in the Bible or the Bible *as* Word. (Lutherans are nervous about any language that says the Bible "contains" the Word of God, making it a vessel and not the stuff that matters.)

The purpose of the Old Testament, the scriptures that Jesus had studied as a Jew, was to be searched because in these scriptures we "have eternal life," yet we find this only when we find him (John 5:39). In the Gospel of John (20:31) the purpose is clear: "These [signs] are written so that [we] may come to believe that Jesus is the Messiah, the Son of God, and that through believing [we] may have life in his name."

11. Why Is the Bible Considered an Authority for the Church?

In some Holy Communion liturgies the congregation sings a question and an answer, both based on a Gospel story: "Lord, to whom shall we go? You have the words of eternal life?" (John 6:68 RSV). It is possible to sing that unthinkingly, if one has sung it often. Singing it "thinkingly" helps pose the issue sharply. Yes, to whom other than Jesus should "we," the congregation, the disciples, go? Who else has the words of eternal life?

Carry that over to the question of the authority of the Bible. Now it is not "to whom" but "to which source" shall we go? Lutherans make much of the ancient creeds and the Lutheran Confessions, but they have no authority except that which is derived from and connects with Scripture. If such sources were about Caesar or Shakespeare, we will probably find them interesting at the Caesar Club or Shakespeare Society meetings, but they have nothing directly to do with "the words of eternal life." The Bible claims to be and we respond: it does. There is nowhere else to go.

At the same time, Lutherans also see human learning, the sciences and history, literature and philosophy, and practical knowledge as potentially gifts of God because they enrich life and perhaps make us more alert human beings to respond to the Bible. We might be grateful for the United States Constitution or some other such documents in other nations, but their services expire with the end of empire or our personal death. They have nothing to do with "the words of eternal life."

Since the Bible is a unique work, it has a unique place. Lutherans do not draw a sharp line or build a high wall between the Bible and all other forms of authority, which are to be seen as "mere" traditions. Tradition comes from the words "handing down," and the handing down from the apostles or the generations to our own time can be heartening evidence of God's continuing work in the world. It may and does speak highly of the value of our experience of God through prayer and hymn singing, meditation and devotion, and charitable activity. It can confirm or support "the words of eternal life," but it is not these.

Church congregations and bodies, including Lutheran church bodies, possess certain kinds of authority. We voluntarily assent to deliberate, vote, and follow outcomes of the vote so long as they do not directly conflict with the Word of God. But, as the Reformers reminded us, church councils do err. They decree or vote or judge one way and some years later they may have to repeal or studiously forget what they voted and once said. They can be marvelous deliberative bodies, arenas in which the Holy Spirit works among consecrated people, settings where those with talents to govern and be agents have their place. They do not "have" the words of eternal life except when they are quoting Scripture.

One New Testament author, writing when the Scriptures were what we call the Old Testament, says that "all scripture is inspired by God and is useful . . ." (2 Timothy 3:16), and Christians accept the New Testament equally as having the authority that comes with divine inspiration. "Lord, to whom shall we go?" "Lord, where else shall we get authority?" In the end, because in the Bible come "the words of eternal life," it is the supreme authority or, in language Lutherans like, the "source and norm" of Christian teaching.

12. Since We Have the New Testament, Why Do We Need the Old Testament?

We could begin to answer this question by shifting it a bit: even if we did not "need" the Old Testament, we would and should want it. Whenever someone asks why we don't jettison the Old Testament, a good question to ask is, "Have you ever read it?" A scholar once wrote a book called *The Enjoyment of Scriptures*. Enjoy! What a novel concept, one might think, until one has tasted the Old Testament.

Don't we need and don't we enjoy the Old Testament? Can we picture getting along without the Twenty-third Psalm or the wonderful language of prophets like Isaiah? Admittedly, because the Old Testament is a record of some really ghastly events, there are in it ghastly pages. No one would rate the book of Judges with the Psalms, in the matter of either enjoyment or need. Yet somehow the stories that reveal human evil fit into the plot wherein God does not give up on God's children, on Israel. We think of the wonders of Old Testament texts in Handel's *Messiah*, in the mysteries of the creation stories and the poems in Job.

Enough. We also *need* the Old Testament because without it the New Testament makes little sense. The Old Testament—

many like to call it the "Hebrew Scriptures"—provides numerous images taken up in the New, such as that of the serpent lifted up in the wilderness, the manna that falls down from heaven, the curse of anyone who is hanged upon a tree, the blessing to the nations, the Suffering Servant of Isaiah and the application of its picture to Jesus' suffering in Jerusalem—all at the heart of the biblical plot.

In the earliest church a heretic named Marcion tossed the Old Testament away, but once he started cutting, he had to throw away much of the New as well. Some still want to join him, because they think the Old Testament is only a book of laws, or the book of the law of God, and we are saved by the gospel. Yet the law in its depth speaks to us. Others, as in Hitler's Germany, rejected the Old Testament as a book of and by and for Israel, and they were anti-Semites. By doing without the Old Testament, they would not know what to make of the word in the Fourth Gospel, "Salvation is from the Jews" (John 4:22).

Christians believe that God, who in older times spoke through the prophets, in the latter days spoke through his Son. Jesus' own spiritual home was the scriptures of the Old Testament. Throwing them away leaves us homeless, since we also live there—or should. We are privileged to do so.

13. Are There Errors in the Bible?

Oh-oh!" we are tempted to say. We have been sailing blithely along through and past some ordinary controversial topics, and then comes this stumper. It *is* a stumper, a disturber of the peace, a potential clouder of thought, as the dropping of a puck at center ice in hockey, so fighting can begin. Here swing the sticks!

Why? Because it often happens that both within Lutheranism and beyond it wherever Christians gather and come to disagreement, one faction accuses the other of not doing justice to the Bible or of treating it as having errors.

Are there errors in the Bible? If we think of what we usually mean with the word "errors," the most helpful answer would be to say, That's a strange question to put to or about the Bible. It is clearly not written to be a scientific textbook or an encyclopedia of history. Curricular counselors advise that you do not go to the back of an algebra book for answers to problems in French grammar. So if in the Gospels we find the measure of miles between Jerusalem and Emmaus or Bethlehem and your odometer has a slightly different reading, it is not important to adjust the odometer or get into an argument about where the trails ran. You get the point whether the distance is six or eight kilometers or miles.

The Gospels sometimes have two accounts of an incident and they don't quite match. Thus Jesus ascends from two different mountains in two different Gospels. Does this mean that it would be important to rerun the tape and get a literal reading of one or the other? He ascended; he is no longer a physical presence among the Twelve in Jerusalem or Galilee. With the story we witness that he is the exalted Lord of the universe, a presence everywhere.

Sometimes people who get stuck on this question claim that the original manuscripts had no errors in them, but copyists introduced some through their sloppiness. It happens that the ancients did provide many different readings, as evidenced in the footnotes in the Greek New Testament, which even fundamentalist seminarians see daily and know about. If the originals were without error and all we have are error-filled, have we any security? Did God fail us by providing us only with messed-up copies? Are we "saved" by the knowledge that somewhere a scroll with Paul's handwriting is waiting to be found?

Luther, who ranks second to none in his awe of the full authority of the Scriptures, readily found and acknowledged "errors." He could fight over the single word "is" in the words of Jesus concerning his body in the Lord's Supper so vehemently that his argument blocked chances for early Protestants to come together. Yet he could see Matthew ascribing a quotation to the wrong prophet, Paul using a failed analogy, or Old Testament writers getting accounts of kings and their histories wrong—and it did not faze him one bit. He seemed to enjoy pointing out these apparent contradictions on the way to saying and showing that whatever the Scriptures say about our salvation is sure.

It could be that the error we make is when we worry about "errors" in the Bible. The impulse to get it all right is understandable, since being responsive to Scripture is an urgent issue. The Holy Spirit guides us to pose better questions, such as how does this text relate to us today?

14. How Do Lutherans Interpret the Bible?

The first thing to acknowledge is that Lutherans—*all* Lutherans—*do* interpret the Bible. Some church bodies and movements were organized around the idea that they "took it straight," that they literally had an absolutely right grasp of the simple gospel, uninterpreted. One has to mourn that they miss a lot—and misinterpret the Bible—by thinking it is not interpreted.

Let's sort this out. First of all, unless we think in Hebrew, Aramaic, or Greek frameworks and languages, and rely instead on English or Spanish or German translations, we are already involved with someone's interpretation. Ask anyone who teaches or studies English as a second language, or overhear first-generation immigrants despairing over attempts to help you get the joke or get inside an idiom they have just used. They have to look for equivalents, which means they interpret by paraphrasing. And we enjoy and learn from such. The Italians had a saying that the translator is inescapably a traitor. We like accuracy in translations, but they are necessarily interpretations.

Second, we interpret in the light of our experiences. A child with an abusive father needs to have the biblical words about God the Father interpreted. People in New Guinea who did not know lambs but had pigs were served by interpretation when the translation "Behold the pig of God, who takes away the sin of the world" landed on them. Sufferers of persecution interpret texts about suffering differently than do suburbanites in their ease. A couple celebrating a golden anniversary after having read a chapter of the Bible every day will interpret passages distinctively: ask any woman if you are a man, or any man if you are a woman.

I come now to the question of how Lutherans *as* Lutherans interpret the Bible. So far I have talked about individuals, but we interpret in company, in community. So as Lutherans listen to the ways African Pentecostals or Russian Orthodox Christians provide angles and highlights, so they listen to Lutherans, who offer their own. Luther, who so often came up with helpful images, said we should interpret the Scriptures as being the manger in which Jesus Christ lies. That was one way of saying that all of the Bible was to be cherished, but also that it had a focus. Begin with Christ and read out from there.

Similarly, Lutherans interpret the Bible—and this goes back to counsel Luther got in the monastery—by moving from the known to the unknown. They interpret not by claiming to understand mysteries in the mind of God, but by following the tracks God leaves in history, the trails of Israel in the wilderness and the Promised Land or of Jesus on the mount for a sermon, or for transfiguration, or for crucifixion. We come to "know" the meanings and interpret the mysteries in the light of what is known.

Lutherans do not treat the sixty-six books of the Bible flatly. They dive right into the letters of Paul, the prophecies and witness of Isaiah, and the Gospel of John and work out from there. Lutherans interpret the Bible by admitting that they and their interpretations are not infallible, but that they occur under the enlightening power and gifts of the Holy Spirit.

15. Do Lutherans Believe in a Literal Adam and Eve?

A nswer: Some do, but why do you ask? It certainly is a natural question, because Adam and Eve come up so early in the plot of the Bible. Some Christians resolve to read all the way through the Bible and often don't get much past Adam and Eve, so they have to make up their minds about them.

The main problem here may not be "Adam and Eve" but what we mean by "literal." That usually gets translated to "If a newspaper reporter were on a creek bank near the Euphrates one morning in such-and-such B.C., would she have seen God "literally" sculpt a human and appear visibly to blow breath into the clay? Given how suspicious we have become of newspaper reporters and their lack of objectivity, we may be better off not picturing that in a quest for security. The impulse to seek the literal does signal seriousness about the Bible and questions of faith, but it is not likely to be satisfied among most believers, Lutherans among them.

Let Christian A, who has literal figured out, and Christian B, who does not, deal with the same stories the same way. Assume both are coming in faith and want to know more not about how the world began—Genesis 1–11 does not tell that—but how God's people became God's people, and what the story of Adam and Eve has to reveal about that. Assume also that they will not be snide and dismissive of the other's approach. Let them approach the Bible story humbly, ready to be awed and informed. Now what happens? They will both marvel at the story, joining as they will the millions of readers, the thousands of commentators in Judaism and Christianity, who have not begun to exhaust the potential meanings of this or that text. They may in effect argue about some elements. Thus Augustine said that if God wanted "man" to rule over "woman," God would have taken Eve from Adam's foot. If God had wanted her to rule, God would have taken her from the crown of his head. Since they were to be at each other's side, God took a rib. A feminist may find one thing—possibly offensive—in that, but will wrestle with it as much as if she were a literalist. A literalist may celebrate it literally but have no idea how to put into practice what he has learned from it.

Paul in Romans 5 took the story seriously, whether literally or not, since for him Adam became a "type" for Jesus, who is a "type" for us. Does the type become more or less revealing depending upon how literally it is intended and taken? The issue is pointed: Not "Are Adam and Eve a literal pair?" but, literally, "What does their story mean for everyone who reads it, alone or in community as, in this case, the Lutheran part of the Christian community?"

chapter three

God

16. Can We Prove That God Exists?

No. Don't be silly. If an author says something like, "Don't be silly," to a reader, it is a sign of disrespect. We should take all serious questions seriously. Certainly, thought about the existence of God is natural, in place, potentially worthwhile, and can be productive of other thoughts about God.

The "don't be silly" is rather a condensation of some of the most beautiful pages in the whole Bible, Job 38 and 39, wherein God asks Job many questions. They are all designed to put his questions into perspective. Where was Job when the world was created? What mysteries of nature could he understand, and if he failed with them, how could he understand the mystery of God's existence?

The terse answer no to the question is then not a put-down but a putting-in-perspective. Any proof that we might dream up can easily be refuted by non-dreaming philosophers and maybe even by the child down the block. What would a proof look like? A child imagines that maybe if there would be a huge bright neon sign atop Everest, the highest mountain, that says, "There Is a God," and with it an audio system louder than any before saying, "There is a God," we might be convinced. But the viewers and hearers would likely dismiss it as a public-relations trick, a mass deception.

Maybe the issue has to do with the word "prove." Humans in each culture and generation define what proving something looks like. We tend to relate proof to language that refers to what we can see, touch, taste, hear, or smell. Whatever with our two eyes, ten fingers, one tongue, two ears, and two nostrils we can grasp is absurdly limited, as are our finite imaginations.

So if we can use words like "silly" and "absurd," then why say, as I have, that our thoughts about this can be worthwhile? Consult a pastor, teacher, catechist, or professor who will report on how she or he rattles off the "proofs" of the existence of God to a class of inquiring disciples and potential new members of a believing community. Hear that the rattling off was to suggest that the proofs are worthless—"But let's go through them anyhow."

So the teacher reports on five classic proofs that depend on logic and observation of the outer world and the inner conscience. Almost always some serious person will come up after the class and say something like, "Why did you dismiss the proofs? Why did you shoot past them?" And then this inquirer will say, "Slow down and repeat them again. One of them hit the nail on the head for me; it cleared some debris, removed a roadblock"—the metaphors keep tumbling.

Why? Because we humans do tend to clutter our minds and confuse our senses and may fail to take note of arguments and probes that do address what has stood in the way of witness to God. St. Thomas Aquinas, the smartest of all the "almost provers" centuries ago, wrote a huge summary book that looked as if it was going to show the author's self-satisfaction at having proven God's existence. But then he stopped short and did not finish it off or close things in. He knew that the proofs make sense only where there is some sort of faith, and the faith makes more sense if one thinks about things like proofs.

Still, the answer to "Can we prove that God exists?" remains simply no.

17. How Can We Know God?

We can know *about* God simply by reading the Scriptures. Knowing *about* God is not the same as *knowing* God. Being told what love is and even being told that some other human somewhere is likely to love us is not the same as hearing from a beloved, "I love you!" and experiencing actions that go with love. So knowing about God could mean being told that God is and that somehow God is likely to love us. That is not the same as recognizing God as the "Thou" or experiencing God's recognizing us as a "Thou." A great Jewish philosopher, Martin Buber, once wrote that God is to be addressed, not expressed. God is known when God is addressed and God addresses us.

There is no point in overrestricting the response to this question any more than in doing so to the previous one. We humans need all the help we can get. God gave us reason and senses, and we are to use them. Martin Luther in the Lutheran confessional writings says that there are enough evidences of God that even "heathen" who do not believe can "know" enough to be able to respond and to be responsible in moral affairs. He is reworking words of St. Paul in the first chapter of Romans. Paul, however, clearly and Luther emphatically say that such knowledge in a person's reason and conscience is not "saving" knowledge. Luther even says that some knowledge of God can be present in other religions. It may help us be responsible in moral life, but it is not a means of bringing people to God.

Saying that this knowledge comes from the Scriptures alone does not mean that it is restrictive, to use the word that came up a moment ago. The Scriptures open us up to the boundless, to the mystery of God, to that which is beyond imagining. And it also is intimate, bringing the God of the heavens into the story of a people, Israel, and into our churches, our chambers, and the chambers of our hearts.

Can "tradition" be a means of knowing God? Roman Catholic, Eastern Orthodox, and some Protestant thought makes a point of saying that it can. Lutherans don't disbelieve it, but they want to do some redefining before they accept such a formula. They want to guard against having *traditions*, lest repeated and long-term ways of doing things get too much credit as helpers. Many really bad habits and teachings get passed on as traditions. The word "tradition" comes from the Latin and means "that which is handed down."

Here it can be of help. Singing some hymns, participating in a liturgy, or receiving the bread and wine of Holy Communion, as believers have done through the centuries and by the millions today, can inspire reflection that makes God's existence vivid. Speaking in prayer and "hearing" a response becomes another kind of proof.

The "sure thing" about coming to know God is when God reaches us in the humility of Jesus Christ, who said, "Whoever has seen me has seen the Father [Abba]" (John 14:9). Here the heart responds. The great mathematician and philosopher Blaise Pascal said that the heart has its reasons that reason cannot know. The heart's reasons can be most profound when it comes to knowing God—even as they do not ask us to forget about ordinary reason, which can be of extraordinary value as we think things through.

18. What Is the Trinity?

This is one of the most basic and certainly most difficult but necessary ways to speak of the God of Christian faith. There is no way of ducking the difficulty or coming to the limits of what pondering it can mean for all of life. We baptize "in the name of the Father and of the Son and of the Holy Spirit." We pronounce benedictions and make the sign of the cross on ourselves or in the face of a congregation in that name. So it is in place to ponder it.

First, think of the difficulties. St. Augustine, the greatest writer on the subject, said that the terms and definition are not very good; they represent our best attempt to say something instead of nothing. We know how hard it is to discuss this theme in any culture, including our own, in which people think differently from the way they did when the terms were first fashioned eighteen centuries ago. We joke about how hard the Trinity is to translate, without always realizing that we are outsiders to the terms and concepts—but not the reality!—of what it expresses.

We can warm to the subject by disarming and being light-hearted at first. For example, a missionary told of his efforts to explain the Trinity to a serious adult in Japan, who had never heard of anything close to it. When told that Christians are thoroughly monotheistic, that is, they adore one God, but that this God comes as "three persons," the man said, "Now I understand. You are ruled by a committee." Another, as he heard of biblical stories connecting the Holy Spirit with the form or presence of a dove, as in the story of the baptism of Jesus, resignedly said, "Honorable Father I understand. Honorable Son I understand. But honorable bird I do not understand at all."

Preachers who celebrate the Holy Trinity sometimes confess that they are stumped on Trinity Sunday as they wrestle with biblical texts and try in fifteen minutes to preach what whole libraries of books cannot satisfactorily address. Some will resort to visual aids, for example, by reproducing the three-leaved (one leaf!) shamrock that St. Patrick was said to have used to help him explain the theme, but they are then told that it is not a satisfactory image.

Or one can be philosophically fancy and deduce that the teaching points to the fact that in one mode or presence or person God comes as Father; in another, as Son; in still another, as Holy Spirit. At once some insider who is attuned to such things will spit out a string of adjectives and nouns that put you in your place but do not help you. You will learn that you're a "modalistic Monarchian," perhaps with a Sabellian or Patripassianist nuance (these were ancient variations of interpretations that came to be rejected). And you will have the right to say, "Get real! I am struggling."

We think of what the teaching of the Trinity aims to protect. This term or concept helps make it possible to address one God, not three and more. It tries to condense teachings from the Bible about how God is revealed and how we experience God. Christians cannot conceive of having a full address to God that does not begin with the Creator. God does not reach us except through the Son. The Holy Spirit reaches us through the Scriptures. The ancient church did us little favor by drawing on the Greek term *hypostasis*, which we have to translate as "person." The important point is to see Father, Son, and Holy Spirit perfectly united, not to be confused with each other, all equal, and—this point was always important—indicating that within the deity there is relation, a model for all of our existence.

Augustine tried out such a model of this relation that helped some and throws us back to the theme of "the Word." Thus in the Trinity God in three persons is the Speaker, the Spoken, and the Hearer. And we relate.

19. What Are Some Practical Results of Believing in the Trinity?

That's a good modern question. It is modern because we and our contemporaries like to be practical, to find a use for everything including here, even a name for God or a name that helps us hear and respond to God. Not all Christians at all times and in all places would be that utilitarian. Mystics, meditators, monks and nuns, pious devotionalists, people whom most of us picture as not having their feet on the ground but who spend most of the time most of their lives "contemplating," are perfectly happy just to let witness to the Trinity *be*, not *be for*. They have minds and imaginations in which they can be perfectly happy pondering or worshiping the Trinity, just as most of us can go deeply into and draw enjoyment out of a piece of music or a work of art. But what practical use is it?

Happily, there *are* practical uses for belief in and speaking of the Trinity.

For example, like all names it helps us grasp for someone and address that one. One person said that by thinking about God without reference to biblical revelation and this creedal form, God was "nothing more than a vague oblong blur." It is practical to let knowledge of what the Trinity points to direct our worship, theology, and lives.

Second, as mentioned before, in a world where a human is tempted—as individualists and some New Age fans are trained to do—to think of themselves as God, or to worship the God within, or to be self-made and therefore tempted to worship the creator, namely, one's self, witness to the Trinity takes us outside ourselves and throws us into relation, into community, into the company not only of the self but of the "other." The key word again is "relational." The Trinity is the model of the relational life, and invoking the Trinity draws us into thinking and experiencing divine-human relations that we can then carry into human-to-human relations.

Witness to the Trinity is also practical because it is enriching. The Bible has marvelous words for the three "persons" in the relational Godhead (and "Trinity," let us confess, is not close to being one of them). God. Father. Creator. Son. Redeemer. Savior. Spirit. Advocate. Comforter. Making "practical" use of the Trinity opens the door of imagination and the focusing power of prayer to much more than if we do not invoke the Trinity.

20. What Is the Providence of God?

Providence: What a wonderful word. Unfortunately, if you hover around Lutherans, you will not hear it often. You can look for it with word search on a computer or in the index to the big fat book of Lutheran Confessions, and you won't find any more than "Providence. See Foreknowledge." "Foreknowledge" references do not get us very far, except to warn us not to confuse it with God's eternal election, which we probably were not doing anyhow. More positively, we are reminded that it "extends over all creatures, good and evil," but is "not the cause of evil" and sets limits on it. It is also not the cause of contempt for the Word. That's it. It is clear that the sixteenth-century Lutherans did not need the word "providence" and that what they were fighting over then may not match what we are curious about now.

Correction: The Lutheran writings *do* witness to Providence, but in the form of verbs. Those who get to memorize key parts of Luther's Small Catechism (highly recommended!) will read and then tuck away wonderful words explaining the First Article of the Creed or the work of the first person of the Holy Trinity. (See, as the previous question and answer suggested, the Trinity is already of practical use!) We read that God "has given me and still preserves my body and soul with all their powers." Now, in addition, God "provides me with food and clothing . . . and all I need from day to day." Third, God "protects me in time of danger and guards me from every evil." "Preserving" and "providing" are acts of Providence, undeserved from a merciful God.

While Lutheran encyclopedias and indexes are sketchy and skimpy, others relish the word. The Founding Fathers of the United States—Washington, Adams, Jefferson, Franklin and most of the rest—used it because they did not want to get too close to the Bible's names for God and wanted to be rather abstract and impersonal and fair to all religions while not offending the non-religious. Within Christianity, Calvinists, who are more at home with "election" and "predestining" and "foreknowledge," are also more ready to speak of Providence. And they make good "practical" use of it.

So may Lutherans and all other Christians. If you detect a certain nervousness about the concept here, it results from a Lutheran fear about humans claiming and knowing too much about the purposes of God. Two cars head home from a party; one takes one route and the other takes another. A train kills those in one and spares those in another. So survivors are tempted to speak of how "Providence" protected them. That is not much comfort or helpful as an explanation to survivors of those killed.

Americans like to say that Providence has taken care of this nation. Does that mean that when we have lost wars or fallen into a Civil War or undergone economic depressions or experienced Katrinas, God's providence was withdrawn and we have to figure out or, worse, explain why God acted as God did? Jesus would have little of that. In one little story, asked about such a question, he threw back a question: when the tower of Siloam fell on some people, he asked, had they been worse sinners than others? No, they happened to have been standing where a tower fell, and the fall was lethal (Luke 13:1–4). Some of that kind of common sense can actually be comforting, and using it can be a first step of returning to the language of how God does "preserve" and "provide."

Jesus speaks of the providence of God in the Sermon on the Mount (Matthew 6:25–33), and elsewhere he said that no sparrow falls without God's knowledge or care (Matthew 10:29). Interpreting Providence works most helpfully, not when we are particular and precise and verging on superstition, but when we see that the whole of creation and all of our lives are under God's care, and that "our lives are hid with Christ in God," who provides.

21. Does God Will Evil and Suffering in the World and in Our Lives?

When such a question arises, it is comforting or would be comforting simply to say no and be done with it. There are many texts in the Bible asserting that God does not will suffering. Christians, including Lutherans who might have a public-relations sense and who desire to make everything come out right and be attractive and salable, have to be honest and, if they are true to the Bible, point to other things it says.

We don't have to like all of what we read as natural humans. If I could tear out one page of the Bible because it looks unacceptable to anyone, it would be part of Isaiah 45:6–7, where Yahweh says, "I am the LORD, and there is no other. I form light and create darkness. *I make weal and create woe.* I the LORD do all these things" (emphasis added). Maybe that's a bad translation. Let's try another: "I make well-being, and I create disaster. I, Yahweh, do all these things" (NJB). A believer recovers sense and faith by focusing on how God will "make weal" and "make well-being" rather than "woe" and "disaster," but the reader responsive to the Bible has to reflect on the tense balancing alternative side of the verse.

Here is one way we can think of it: God the Creator creates out of love. That creation finds us in a created and hence "natural" world, not Eden of old or Paradise of tomorrow or Utopia in between. Since we belong to the created or natural world, we are subject to all that goes with it, including birth and death, springtime and autumn, sunshine and shadow—some lives knowing outrageously more of the latter than of the former. And as we belong to created nature, we also live in a world in which accidents happen, unexplained good and bad things occur. Those people killed by the fallen tower of Siloam just *happened* to be there, and the surviving soldier whom one bullet missed just *happened* to have moved before it came and killed his buddy behind him.

The great and universal mark of belonging to created nature is, of course, death. A prominent physician, Lewis Thomas, addressing an American audience when people spoke so much of the denial of death, said that we will be healthier if we recognize that death exists and will come: "There's an awful lot of it going around these days." There may be more than six billion people on the earth now, almost all of them replacements for those who died a little more than one hundred years ago.

Lutherans are taught to be realists, not assigning to God the evil and suffering in our lives except as the Creator who places us in nature and among often stupid humans, including ourselves, who are subject not just to "natural" evil and suffering but to "humanly caused" evil and suffering. If Lutherans are to be realists and find honesty to be the best policy for producing therapy and a positive outlook on whatever may come, they are also to be realistic *hopers*, because of God's love.

I think it's a good guess to say that one of the favorite affirmations in the whole Bible when Lutherans take it off the shelf or turn it over in their minds is from Paul's letter to the Romans (8:38–39): "For I am convinced that neither death, nor life, nor angels, nor rulers, nor things present, nor things to come, nor powers, nor height, nor depth, nor anything else in all creation, will be able to separate us from the love of God in Christ Jesus our Lord." They find that affirmation infinitely more creative as a voice than are the voices of those who know exactly what God had in mind in creating "weal" or "woe."

22. Is God Male?

That is a question that some critics will say could only have come up in modern times when radical feminists influenced Christian thinking. Such a charge does not do justice to Christian history, however, because through the centuries believers—not only women—have pondered the meaning of biblical language in which, yes, masculine pronouns are usually used for God. Read the mystics of the Middle Ages (or modern times), and you will find them often addressing God in feminine terms. So does the Bible itself on occasion, and most of us not only do not lose our cool but are warmed to think of it, when God is revealed as doing "women things." These include giving birth, nursing, mothering, and more.

In a time when we are rethinking so many of the ways we speak about divine things, the holy, and God, there are reasons to rejoice at the use of imaginations that revisit old texts, including biblical texts, there to unearth surprises that enlarge our creative horizons and give us more reasons to address God in more ways.

This can be done without wrenching activities of the "in your face" sort, which can show up if elites—some women now against other women and men of all ages—draw lines of offense where they do not serve positive purposes. Listen carefully and you will find that feminine pronouns are often spoken in love and can help steer alienated people, not only women, to the love of God. In turn, one finds good reason to use masculine biblical names when they are deeply rooted and in place.

God is "other." God is "spirit." Therefore all revealed and applied names, however close to the disclosed character of God they are, are inadequate and inaccurate, since they must use human metaphors, analogies, and terms we can comprehend. Much of the revolt against exclusively male conceptions of God and God's activity can result from cultural misunderstandings. Thus in a world in which "men's movements" and "muscular Christianity" and "manliness" and "macho" are celebrated by verbal muscle-flexers, a notice by a Jewish scholar is helpful when she writes that in biblical imagery, God has a "countenance" to lift up and a "holy arm" to lay bare. But the Hebrew Scriptures do not have much interest in God below the belt!

Such scriptures show much interest in God and Spirit and Yahweh-above-the belt and an arm that may be holy and bare and strong, but also soft and crooked so that it can cradle us humans in need of care. Meanwhile, it is in place, say many Lutherans, for members to be patient with each other as we all make our often ungainly ways on roads untrodden and by paths not yet well worn.

P.S. And we can also enjoy the trodden and well-worn ones.

chapter four

Jesus Christ

23. What Is the Incarnation?

Incarnation is one of those church words that people do not use much on the streets. Now and then you will hear of someone being "evil incarnate," but the term won't get you very far at the stock market, in the nursery, or at the football game. That it is such a church word may be in its favor, since it points to and designates something very special, set apart. It comes from the words "in" and "flesh" and means to take on bodily existence. We seldom have occasion to use that word until it comes to Christian talk about God's taking on human flesh and bodily form in Jesus of Nazareth.

Incarnation is both one of the most shocking and most appealing realities in all of Christian imagination and language. It is shocking because it offends opinion to picture that God, the limitless and boundless Other, the Creator of billions of galaxies, the perfection of love, should take on the life of a baby in the Christmas story, the dying criminal in the Good Friday story, and the one raised not as a phantom but as a "spiritual *body*." If it is shocking, it is also appealing, because the incarnation, God's taking on of a form like ours, makes God accessible, available, and approachable.

Scholars who try to figure out what all the early Christian congregations in the New Testament had in common boil it down to something pretty much like this: they believed that *the human Jesus is the exalted Lord.* Christians through the ages have used different languages to witness to this. The New Testament reflects story forms that Hebrew-speaking people used. The writers of Christian creeds did so chiefly in places where people thought in terms that matched those of the Greek philosophers. They talked about "being" and "substance," "natures" and "persons," in ways that are not easy to grasp today—but we cling to them for what they protect and express.

Lutherans accept all the biblical pictures of how divine and human natures both meet in Jesus Christ. Like the creeds, Lutheranism's original documents witnessed mainly that Jesus Christ, who is "true God and true man, who was truly born, suffered, was crucified, died and was buried," is our Lord. Where, one asks, are the parables, the sermons, the healings, the stories of Jesus' lively action in company? They are at the heart of teaching and piety. For the basics, however, the key point is that all the things that matter happen in Jesus Christ, because he is "true God and true man, who was truly born. . . ."

Curiously, this teaching, so hard for minds to grasp, opens the mind after reaching the heart. People crowd Christmas services if not others, because in them the God who often seemed so remote and hard to grasp comes among us in a helpless infant. God's power comes through best in weakness, God's glory in humility, and such forms of power are most clear in witness to Jesus. One scholar has said that Jesus belongs utterly in the world, but moves in it with an otherness that is unmistakable.

Some of that otherness may result from the way Gospel stories are told, but in the end, it is there because Jesus, who is so much one with humanity, also embodies the Other, God. Believers forget their shock and find that appealing.

24. Where Was Jesus Before He Came to Earth?

A little Jewish boy was conceived in the womb of Mary, yet he is also the divine Lord Jesus Christ. Where was he before his birth? We do not ordinarily ask where Beverly or George was before he or she "came" into our midst, being content to track the story back to two parents and by DNA research into ancestry. That is enough for us because we make no special claims that they are "Other," divine in formal senses of the term (even though all parents think that their children are special!).

Our reasoning cannot get us far in answering this question. If biology does not help us, neither does history. Christians, ever since New Testament times, have often read back into the Old Testament, the Hebrew Scriptures, references to a coming "Prince of Peace," but those texts do not say where such a person-to-be was when those scriptures were written. The New Testament writers do not concern themselves much with this question in this form. They know, whether they use the words or not, that God is the Creator of space, the "where" of this question, and of time, the "when" that would go with it, as in "before."

The New Testament does provide some clues, however, particularly in its use of the term *logos* (word). The classic text is John 1: "In the beginning was the Word, and the Word was with God, and the Word was God. . . . And the Word became flesh. . . ." (vv. 1, 14). The Greek word *logos* helped theologians speak of the "preexistence" of Christ, but it did not help them locate this *logos* any "where" but "with God." *Logos* can mean "word," or an "eternal principle," something that points to all the reality there is. We stumble and falter looking for ways to express this.

As with so many concepts of this sort, the helpful question is, what *use* is the witness to the *logos*, the preexistent Christ, the Word that was with God and was God and is now among us? The Christian creed-makers took it up with zest. Thinking in such terms helps assure that Jesus is not cut down to human size and left there. In the early church one of the greatest threats was a party of followers of Arius, who considered that the Son had not come from eternity but had a beginning, in which case he had to be subordinate to the Father.

That word "nothing but" is a good signal here: witness to Jesus as *logos*, second person of the Trinity, somehow preexistent before Bethlehem, is the great enemy of what someone calls "nothing buttery." The *logos* locates him with God and as God, so there is no "nothing but" but rather there is "everything" in him. If our minds force us to think in terms of space and time, and thus do us a service, they would in this case lead us to say, "If we have to ask where Jesus Christ as *logos* was before he came into the world, look at the face of God."

Lutherans have not really tried to get a patent on the teaching of "Jesus before he came to the world," but are quite happy with the stumbling but still creative efforts of the creed-writers of long ago.

25. Do Lutherans Believe in the Virgin Birth of Jesus?

Why do you ask? Answer that and the answers to the question itself become clear. Start with affirmations: Yes, Lutherans believe in the virgin birth of Jesus, because the Gospel of Luke speaks of it. Yes, they speak of it at least weekly when they recite their oldest creed, the Apostles', which states that Jesus was "born of the virgin Mary." That phrase was not designed to say that "virgin" is her first name. Yes, Lutherans believe in the affirmation, but their original writings do not make much of it. They have other stresses: that Jesus, "Mary's son," is born of "the pure virgin," "the most blessed virgin," "the Mother of God," is the stress, not the biological and chemical processes of conception.

Why do you ask? The question has gotten tense, because in the twentieth century, as Christians fought over ways to regard

Christian teaching, one party thought the way to solve everything was with the word "literal." Do you believe in the *literal* second coming of Christ, the *literal* virgin birth? Say yes, and you were clear. Say more, and you were in trouble. What starts out as a great hymn celebrating in story form the way in which Jesus was different becomes a trip-wire, a test to determine "who's in and who's out."

Huge battles erupted in the middle of the previous century over the Revised Standard Version of Isaiah 7:14, in which *almah* was "young woman" and not "virgin," since with "virgin" there could have been one Old Testament reference to bolster the two references to the virgin birth in the New Testament (Matthew 1:18–25; Luke 1:34–35). Generations trained in microbiology included men and women of great faith who could not bring their imaginations around to see why this "literal" theme was to be the test of their faith. So, if admitted to membership, they readily and willingly recited the creed and boisterously read or sang the *Magnificat*, "Mary's song" (Luke 1:46–55). They had an insight understood by great theologians in the new time: that affirming the virgin birth is one way, a storied way, to point to the mystery that Jesus was among us as someone "Other," God's Son—and that this teaching is a way of enhancing that faith. So most Lutherans will not cross their fingers when they imagine their way into what this means and say, "Yes, I believe. . . ."

26. Why Did Jesus Come into the World?

Lutherans tend to accept most of the answers to this question that have been provided through Christian history by men and women who wanted to be faithful to the Bible. We can talk about some of them in a moment. This question, however, provides an occasion to illustrate a characteristic way Lutherans have gone about answering such questions. They do have a characteristic angle of vision, a spin. They take a difficult, far-reaching question, cut it down to size, and bring it home to the person, the individual.

So in the heart of Lutheran teaching, there is one sentence many prefer above all others in this regard. In Luther's Small Catechism the individual—picture a child learning catechism—confesses that Jesus came to work in this world; he has done "all this . . . that I may be his own, live under him in his kingdom, and serve him in everlasting righteousness, innocence, and blessedness, just as he is risen from the dead and lives and rules eternally." "All this" means that "he has redeemed me . . . [and] freed me."

In the Large Catechism the same idea appears: "He became a human creature . . . so that he might become Lord over sin. . . . And he did all this so that he might become my Lord. For he did none of these things for himself, nor had he any need of them." So the answer is this: Jesus came into the world as an act of divine generosity, holy selflessness, and concern for the creature—and not just for humanity in general but to get the full brunt of real human life—for me.

Theologians have elaborated on Jesus' incarnation in libraries full of books. Luther said it was the most important teaching. In the Middle Ages a great theologian, Anselm, wrote *Cur Deus Homo?* (*Why Did God Become a Human?*). In it he tried to condense long and complex teachings. His answer, which involves the medieval emphasis on "satisfaction," reflected issues that disturbed people in his day and do not quite match Lutheran and contemporary ways of thinking. In Luther's Europe, people often thought of God's dealing with them as an accountant would, someone who as bookkeeper kept track of our sins, errors, flaws, and violations. Tit for tat: "we" did bad things, and the good God demanded that we make up for them. We owed more than we could pay, however. Someone had to "make satisfaction" for our debts. They were so huge that no ordinary human could begin to satisfy God—"satisfy" is the key word. So Jesus had to come into the world to make satisfaction for us.

Undeniably there are scriptural references to satisfaction. Lutheran writings and preaching make allusions to it, and in the past in some places it became a central emphasis. Since most of us don't think of God the way Anselm did, however, we have looked to other biblical resources to answer this question. Jesus came into the world to bring about an exchange: the God who raised him from the dead "exchanged" his situation for ours—we get the riches that he left behind in order to become human and he took on the flaws we bore as humans.

He came into the world to assure victory over the enemies of God as they appear in our communities and among us. He came into the world to bring light to the dark places of our hearts and world. He came to call for faith, to spread love, to instill hope. At root, "All this he has done that I may be his own" is a Lutheran way of condensing the whole catalog of answers.

27. Why Did Jesus Have to Die?

The fact that we began to answer this question while reflecting on the previous one, "Why did Jesus come into the world?" and that the two questions and their answers overlap suggests something about Christian ways of talking about Jesus Christ and his work. It is in some ways overstating the case to collapse the meaning of Jesus' coming into the act that seals our relation to God, his death. One can almost hear the words of the Christmas carol telling that Jesus has "come for to die, for poor ordinary people like you and like I."

He was born to die.

Admittedly, that condensation leaves out so very much, and Lutherans have sometimes accused themselves of skipping too fast from Christmas to Good Friday. Some of their thinkers have welcomed the fact that in the official creed-like writings the words skip quickly from virgin birth through suffering to death and resurrection. Stop! Where is the rest of his story and of Bible history?

Here we need help from some other Christians who stress the life and work of Jesus and do not hurry to the death, though the death gives meaning to it all. One Baptist theologian did a favor by writing a book titled *Saved by His Life*. He showed how many people in the Gospels were "saved"—healed, cured, taught, ennobled, rescued—because of the ways he dealt with them, before his death and perhaps in anticipation of his death, but in and during and "by" his life.

Yes, he came to die, but he also came to teach. Whoever loves the Christian story is glad for the fact that Jesus came as a storyteller. We relish the stories of the good Samaritan and the prodigal son. He came to preach, to set examples, to offer cheer and company, to admonish and judge—and we are immeasurably better off for all of them. Yet Lutherans are in the company of those who admit that there have been plenty of good storytellers and healers. What makes Jesus' "other things" meaningful has to do with "the main thing" that he did: he died.

It is not easy and perhaps not really possible to explain with complete satisfaction why the story had to go that way. In children's sermons we find little ones responding to Jesus but certainly not catching on to his "making satisfaction" of their sins, though aware of sins they may be. The story appears against the background of the Old Testament, where a scapegoat took part. Or another where Moses lifted up a bronze serpent on a tree, which Christians see as prefiguring Jesus on the cross. Anselm was not totally off the point: humans did and do owe a great debt to God that they cannot satisfy, and Jesus came to make the change.

Jesus had to die, finally, because death for another is the final and utter guarantee of the integrity of a person and an act. "No one has greater love than this," Jesus says, than "to lay down one's life for one's friends" (John 15:13). His need to die was to show that there were no limits to his love, that with us and our need in mind he could stand among the evil ones who thought they were getting a victory. In Lutheran thought these evil "ones" are sin, death, and the devil. His death, however, tricks them and takes away their victory and bragging rights. This is so because God vindicates Jesus by raising him from the dead. In the whole biblical plot and in the mood of this question and answer, "God raised Jesus because God had to."

28. What Is the Meaning of the Cross?

You see the cross in gold or diamonds dangling from a chain around the neck. It serves as a kind of decoration when those who put church papers together have some white space to fill but little time to find art. The cross appeared on the banners of the Crusaders who went to win back from Muslims the holy places of Jerusalem but ended up killing Eastern Christians and sometimes each other. The cross appears as "old, rugged," at some places, on mountaintops at others. Children sometimes have used a luminous cross to focus their bedtime thoughts to sleep peacefully. The hymnal is full of references to the cross of Christ in which we glory.

The cross is two pieces of wood, put together in such a way that, if you are a Roman, you can tie or nail victims to it, exposing it to the elements and the vultures, so that the person on it will suffer the most agonizing and humiliating death imaginable.

You can hang Jesus on it.

Christians hang many meanings on the cross. Paul wanted to be known as preaching nothing but Christ and him crucified. In the main church in Wittenberg, Luther's hometown, there is a painting by Lukas Cranach in which on the right Luther is seen preaching, on the left is a congregation that includes a picture of his wife and son, and between them is Jesus on the cross. Lutheran pastors often mount this picture on their study walls as a reminder that they should never look out at a congregation without seeing it in the light of the cross.

The cross is a symbol, a reference to a historic act, and a conveyer of meaning. Lutherans connect it, as do so many other Christians, with acts that they call "atonement." The New Testament has no single teaching on it, and the church has never defined a doctrine of it. We already have mentioned the ways in which the gift of Jesus on the cross effects a victory and can be seen as a sacrifice or substitute for others.

The cross stands for the fact that Jesus' death was vicarious, not just his own death; he was the "vicar" or "representative" for all humanity. In the Fourth Gospel Jesus refers to that story of Moses lifting up the serpent in the wilderness, for healing, and says of the cross, "I, when I am lifted up from the earth, will draw all people to myself" (John 3:14; 12:32). If we had only a book of moral sayings by Jesus, we would shelve it with other moralists' writings and ignore it. We are "drawn" by this act.

Sometimes Jesus is described as the mirror of the fatherly heart of God. On the cross we see mirrored that parental heart, that love that attracts, that is meant for all and will not let us go. You can easily forget the words that end with "-ation," such as expiation, propitiation, justification, reconciliation—all of which, believe it or not, are talking about what is made so clear in the story and symbol of the cross. You cannot forget the cross.

29. Did Jesus Really Rise from the Dead, and What Does His Resurrection Mean?

Take the second part of this question first, since it motivates us to get back to the first. Lutherans, focused by the biblical writer on whom they draw most, Paul the apostle, have no doubt about the meaning of the resurrection. They can put this negatively as he did: we are just fooling around, biding and wasting time, picking second-rate authors for reading, going through the motions of piety, "if Christ is not raised." Or, most clearly, "If Christ has not been raised, your faith is futile and you are still in your sins" (1 Corinthians 15:17). Consider that a rather emphatic and decisive statement. We think of few more depressing options than the one with which Paul follows up: "If for this life only we have hoped in Christ, we are of all people most to be pitied."

Since Christ is risen "on the third day," Lutherans join all fellow-believing Christians in blowing the trumpets, bellowing the hymns, ringing the bells, and greeting each other, "Christ is risen!" "Christ is risen indeed. Hallelujah."

The resurrection means that God vindicates Jesus. One Lutheran hymn has put Good Friday radically: "O sorrow dread.

Our God is dead." That is, God pours everything into the life of God's Son, Jesus Christ. Apparently abandoned on the cross, he shouts, "My God, my God, why have you forsaken me?" (Mark 15:34). But he is raised to new life, never to be abandoned again, in his glory, and now none of us ever have to be abandoned.

Back to the first part of the question: "Did Jesus really rise from the dead?" That "really" suggests some nervousness: "Did Jesus rise from the dead?" does not convey the anxiety people have about what happened and what they are to believe. Pour on the anxiety: "Did Jesus really, *really* rise from the dead?"

Lutherans join Christians of all sorts and with special emphasis when they answer yes, for theirs is an Easter faith. They might have been virtuosos at being penitent, confessing, being down and being glum, as many picture some of their cultures of long ago. Now, however, they have not caught on if they are not at the head of the procession of those who receive the gift of victory because of Christ and draw new life from their identification with him.

Did he really rise? Some people think "really" means that God had to take every cell of his dead body and physically reconstitute it. The Bible does not speak in those terms. Paul and other writers fumble as they look for words to deal with this. Clearly we are dealing with a phenomenon that we do not reduce to biological or physical explanation. We still do best with Paul's approach. He does not say, "People get raised all the time, and this is one more resurrection." No, he says that it is a new creation, something without precedent or analogy, though it will have consequences—in our identification and resurrection with him.

What really happened was not the result of wishful thinking, make-believe stories, illusion or delusion, sleight of hand or trickery. Jesus walked among the disciples after his death and also, Lutherans believe, is present in their baptism, at the table, in the preached and spoken and sung words—present, *alive* among them today.

chapter five

Humanity

30. What Is the Purpose of Human Life?

Lutherans are not programmed to be arrogant, and it is easy to be arrogant and unhelpful when setting out to spell out the purpose and meaning of life. No doubt everyone has times when such purpose is hard to find. Shattering experiences occur, as in wars that slaughter millions of innocents, as did several wars in the century past. Where is the meaning of life when an adolescent on whom parents lavished much care goes to the wrong parties, hangs out with the wrong crowd, gets on methadone, and sees her brain virtually dissolve, so she will live a short and mean life? Where is the purpose for those who live lives of quiet desperation or fall into profound clinical depression? In all such circumstances, it would be a flip, cruel, and stupid assertion for someone to say that she has everything figured out.

Nor do Lutherans deride people who find meaning and purpose in life apart from faith in God, through various disciplines and philosophies. It may be hard to conceive of this, if one's life is centered in God. Yet there are many people who are generous, sacrificial, empathic, and often joyous as they serve others and find purpose in doing so on purely humanitarian grounds.

And yet, and yet . . . Lutherans do not believe that durable and profound answers to the questions of meaning and purpose are fulfilled apart from reference to God. St. Augustine, a kind of grandfather-in-faith to Lutherans in his *Confessions*, talks to God and says, "You have made us for yourself, and our hearts are restless until they find their rest in you." Philosopher Merleau-Ponty has said, "Because we are present to a world, we are condemned to meaning." We would go mad (or are mad) if everything comes at us as chaos, plotless, a kaleidoscopic set of impressions. We are "condemned to meaning," so we need help and welcome help.

For Lutherans, the words at the end of comment on the First Article of the Apostles' Creed in the Small Catechism are contributions to the answer. Since "I" am made and preserved by God, for all of this "I surely ought to thank and praise, serve and obey him." The Second Article ends with the understanding that "I may be his [Jesus'] own, live under him in his kingdom, and serve him in everlasting righteousness, innocence, and blessedness." Those are good starters.

The thoughtful Lutheran Christian is aware that without a provided "plot," she has to be seen—as a pure materialist sees her—as nothing but atoms and molecules, cells and biological processes. What is more, she is located in a universe so vast that its dimensions do not permit one to make sense, since everything is so grand and remote and impersonal that "I" cannot count.

Over against that come the awareness and the assertion that against all such impressions and conclusions, "I" really do matter. Made by God and cared for by God, won back from my plotless life to "being my Lord's own" puts me on track to begin an exciting search in which meaning gets tested every day and found more often than we deserve.

31. What Does It Mean to Say Humans Are Created in the Image of God?

e would not even ask this question did we not read or hear in the Scriptures that this is so. Yes, we can concentrate on the dignity and beauty of another human and make a judgment that he or she is made in the image of God. But is that a picture we would naturally use?

It is not natural to use such a phrase, because we have not even a glimmer of a hint or a whisper of the notion that God is a carved image, a legged and armed being whose symmetry gets sculpted into our own form. God is spirit, God is invisible, and we find no reason to disagree with such an assertion. To be made in the image of an invisible spirit would be of no help at all. We are stumped.

Then we read on the first pages of the Bible that God made humans "in the image of God." So this image of an image is God's idea, not our own. That awareness can spur us on to see what else is involved. God is a "Thou" who freely chooses to have a dialogue partner, a character in stories, someone to love and by whom to be loved. So in Genesis the conversation gets started within God, as it were, when we read, "Let us make humankind in our image, according to our likeness" (Genesis 1:26).

Still, we are stuck if we want to go about this naturally. The great theologian Karl Barth liked to remind us that in the Bible God is Other, wholly Other, not to be reduced. The Bible goes on for hundreds of pages spelling out what is at stake: the feature of God's likeness that appears in the Genesis story and all that follows is that the human is made to be related to God—and then and thus to others. God craves relation, and so do humans.

The teaching is important because it starts to help us learn to take care of ourselves. Messing up our lives means messing up the possibility that God's image can be reflected in the lives around us. It means robbing ourselves of the dignity God intends for us by making us related beings. Since we do mess up, we need help in further defining the search for meaning and purpose and finding out what has happened to confuse the image of God. It's called sin.

32. What Is Sin?

At last, here is a really short question. It would be nice to have a short answer, but the Bible, the Christian tradition, and the witness and practice of Lutherans ask for more. A short answer: Sin is anything that obscures the image of God in us. Sin is anything we "are" as created humanity born into a world we call "fallen." This meant for Luther and means for Lutherans that however much we like to congratulate ourselves and others, however much we want to encourage "goodness," however little we are interested in judging others, we are short of the mark.

Some years ago Karl Menninger, a psychologist, wrote a book titled *Whatever Happened to Sin?* He had counseled many people who refused to analyze themselves and others sufficiently to see themselves as given over to sin. More recently we find that the concept of sin is obscured by so many books and programs on self-esteem, of God-as-my-self. Many a television program and more books will try to be of help by removing all concepts of sin. I am fine without self-examination or the Other-examination inspired by God.

Such affirmations get followed up with complaints that religion is what messes things up. Christian and, within that tradition, Lutheran ways of looking at the human condition, after a superficial glance, *can* look degrading. Even our better acts don't count for lifting our way up to God. Persons who have trouble with recognizing sin have to be capable of deluding themselves—isn't doing so itself a sin, for starters?

Before we even begin to think of a way out and while still tempted to define humans optimistically and humanistically, we do well to see what advantages there are in realistic views of sin. Such views provide perspective and help ready us for receiving divine help, out of which and after which we can deal with our self-image in awesomely elevated ways.

Until then, it's useful to look at some biblical images of sin; it can mean "missing the mark" or "transgressing the line." Maybe the best Lutheran definition comes from Luther, when he describes a person as *incurvatus in se*, which means "curved in upon oneself." There is no opening through which we can hear a word of criticism after bad actions. No opening exists through which we let ourselves see what others see. There is so much self-preoccupation that we spurn help and want to "fix" sin on our own.

Do an experiment: read one day's worth of newspapers or watch one hour of prime-time news and see whether a definition of the human apart from sin holds up. We live in virtual laboratories where we get close-up studies of sin. Using them can be a part of healing, just as a clinical laboratory is a potential element in healing. Finding out what is wrong with us and why this is so is a first step toward righting, or being righted.

33. Why Do We Sin?

We sin in part because of what Lutherans and others call "original sin." But we have to use that concept with care, because it can be so easily misinterpreted and misused. Some people make a big point of saying that behind original sin is the reality of the devil. Blame the devil. Do something evil and say, "The devil made me do it!" There may be something to the theological proposition about the devil's agency. Lutheran writings regularly locate us as blighted by "sin, death, and the devil," in such ways that "the devil" now appears at the root of all the others. The problem with applying that truth is that it is tailor-made as an all-purpose way of shifting eyes and scrutiny and blame from "me."

Too much accent on sin as occurring because "the devil made me do it" removes one from a zone in which we can get help. If the devil made you do it, just have someone chase the devil away and you are home free. Lutherans are trained in self-examination, and once this has meant locating the devil, the personalized agency of what most thwarts the purposes of God, we turn to the "me," not the fateful "made me."

We sin because we are biological beings who need food and drink and shelter to survive. If we feel that we do not have resources for these or are not first in line to get them, we turn greedy. Watch any line in a store or an agency, and you will see how behavior changes when people think there is a shortage—or how angry they will be when someone "crashes the line." Having much wealth does not remove one from sin, since very well fed and rich and secure people are often the most sinfully greedy.

We are biological beings, and most of us are tempted to misuse the sexual attraction of the other to serve the self. We are social beings, and we may well misuse the role of society. In chapter 2 I mentioned that original sin can be translated as "things are not as they ought to be." Neither sin nor not-as-ought is sufficient by itself. They are only beginnings. Thoughtful people examine themselves to assess what makes them sin. Self-preoccupied people can be so busy examining themselves that they do not see God or the role of the other.

A little story from early Lutheranism: Luther was highly aware of sin and, as his fellow monks said, "scrupulous" about confessing sins. His poor confessor had to listen to Luther for hours as the young monk went mentally digging up almost irrelevant faults, until he said, in a sense, "Get over it—and then we can talk about the good life."

Again, to put it in Lutheran terms, we sin because we are "curved in upon ourselves," which is not the best place to be turned.

34. Do Lutherans Believe That Humans Are Totally Evil?

One word that often got and gets Christians into trouble was picked up somewhere along the way by gloomy sinners or judgmental pastors. They called humans "totally depraved." That word carries a very heavy psychological overtone. Depraved people are sex offenders who prey on people.

Depraved people are those rich who steal from the poor, never letting their consciences in on it. Depraved are sick, sick, sick. We like to think of people as being at least partly healthy.

Instead, we use terms that are cousin to total depravity to say that what is wrong with us reaches all parts of us, "totally." Lutherans had to fight against the notion that we were sinners only in some parts of life: our sexual natures, which turn out to bring forth the most glamorous zones for examination. Or we were cheaters and disloyal and slanderers. But then, we were also religious, faithful, good, and, to use today's term, "spiritual," and in that part of our expressions thought we were not sinners.

Wrong, said Luther and the Lutherans. Dietrich Bonhoeffer somewhere said that Martin Luther preferred hearing the angry cry of the outraged or outrageous atheist to the pious prattle of the spiritual. It is often in our being "spiritual" that we work things out in such a way that we don't have to pay any attention to God. The monk at prayer ran a higher risk of being sinful than the marital partners having sex. The message is this: don't be preoccupied with "how bad" we are, how really-really-really bad, but rather notice that all aspects of life are tainted and that we need (as we will get) help.

35. What Do We Mean by "Original Sin"?

I have circled around this term often enough that we might try a different approach here where it is asked so frontally. I referred to original sin as a statement about oneself and all humans in the terms of "things are not as they ought to be," and they cannot be made right on our own, constituted as we are. That constitution is not corrupting or corrupted because of the sexual act in which each person's parents indulged, or during which they enjoyed themselves. Some ancient Christians like Augustine blamed sexuality and procreation most for passing on "bad seed," and Luther sometimes spoke of sexual relations as the means of passing on original sin. There's just enough biblical background for such an assertion that one might at least pay minimal attention to it—but it gets us nowhere, or at least not very far.

However we got there, we "belong to a sinful humanity," which is universal and inescapable and at root the base of what goes wrong in human affairs. This time we will spend a moment looking at what the classic Lutheran documents teach. They are interested in original sin as a condition or situation that keeps God from ruling. To be "without fear of God, without trust in God," means that a force called sin blocks the free passage between us and God (Augsburg Confession 2:1, Latin version).

To make the case extreme: when one locates original sin as blockage "by nature" of what God would effect in us, Lutherans who believe this would like to win any contest that has Christians vying to see who takes original sin most seriously. But then they want to turn this around and insist that because of baptism and by the grace of God, no one can say more positive things about the "new being," the person liberated by God in Christ. Talk about self-esteem: such a person is not only "*as* Christ" but "*a* Christ" to the neighbor, because in repentance and faith that person is situated so that God sees not the "old Adam" of original sin but the "new being" in Christ.

36. Do We Have "Free Will"?

No, has to be the Lutheran answer if one wants to identify with Martin Luther. One of Luther's greatest books is *On the Bondage of the Will*. He was arguing with a great scholar, Erasmus, and both of them overreached in writings well worth reading. We can let Luther take care of his own affairs and then consult his record only where it reaches to help us.

Whenever a complex and uncomfortable Christian teaching comes along, it is profitable to begin by asking what it is out to protect, what limits it is setting. In this case we can begin by saying what the absence of free will is *not*. It is not a claim that we are robots, unable to think for ourselves, decide for ourselves, take responsibility for ourselves. Such notions about limits go against almost everything Christians assert about human responsibility.

Instead, this assertion exists to remove the temptation to think that morally we can do everything we want. Instead, we stand with the apostle Paul, who confessed that the good that he would he did not, and that which he knew he should not, that he did (Romans 7). He was not writing autobiography so much as analyzing the human condition.

When an athlete is elected to the Hall of Fame, we often get a testimony like, "My parents taught me that anything I willed and really worked for, I could attain." No doubt a million other parents said the same thing and half a million kids had just as much will and worked just as hard, but they are not in the Hall of Fame. Such sayings are sort of humble expressions of profound pride. "I did it!" A five-foot-five collegian is not going to become a professional middle linebacker because of will. A pipsqueak-voiced person is not going to get to the Metropolitan Opera stage by willing.

So, morally—and now the case is universal—despite the best of intentions, we *cannot* always make the right decisions and follow them. That is a dangerous-sounding phrase, because it can breed apathy, loss of interest, failure to want to be what God intended us to be. Celebrating the will without claiming that it is simply and absolutely "free"—and freedom of the will means nothing if it is not simply and absolutely free—can be liberating.

Here's why: God takes the broken beings that we are and makes us straight so we can fulfill divine purposes. Lutherans live by such biblical words as, "My grace is sufficient for you, for power is made perfect in weakness" (2 Corinthians 12:9). God plays tricks on the Strong Man, the Super Woman. God works through those who do not matter much in the world. With divine help and mercy, they are free.

It's time to quote a Lutheran charter document, the Augsburg Confession (XVIII.1–2) "A human being has some measure of free will, so as to live an externally honorable life and to choose among the things reason comprehends. However, without the grace, help, and operation of the Holy Spirit a human being cannot become pleasing to God, fear or believe in God with the whole heart, or expel innate evil lusts from the heart."

Humans have all the freedom of the will they need to meet at least minimal standards of moral expectations. It's only where it counts, the free will that effects rightness with God, that will has to be seen as totally limited or, in Luther's phrase, "bound."

In the end, Lutheran teaching on "original sin" is not so much a statement about the human as it is about God, the absence of God, and how God would address the human in need. It turns out that God would meet him or her with liberating rescue. Original sin is a grim and joyless teaching if we use it to concentrate on how morally bad we are, but it is anything but that when it is used to point to how good God is and what God intends to do with messed-up humans, humanity, and "me."

chapter six

The Holy Spirit

37. What Does the Holy Spirit Do?

This question could be one of the hardest yet. However, for Lutherans, if we may speak a bit lightheartedly about it, this one instead is easy. The Holy Spirit is, of course, a mystery, hard to grasp—impossible, for that matter, by nature and definition.

Now, if one begins at the place where Lutherans naturally gravitate, to the Scriptures, there is testimony that can be boiled down. Martin Luther, a great boiler-down in his Small Catechism, is very specific, very precise in describing with a set of verbs what the Holy Spirit does. We cannot do better than to listen, especially since it is addressed to each of us, as if in the first person singular.

The Holy Spirit "has called me through the gospel." The Holy Spirit never works apart from means, is not a flutterer in the air or a kind of aerosol spray of spirituality. The gospel is graspable, since it comes in the form of stories, parables, and announcements of grace, all of which "call" us.

The Holy Spirit "has enlightened me with his gifts." Biblically, the Holy Spirit is also associated with tongues of fire, like the lights on the disciples' heads on Pentecost, and is the bringer of light in the form of "gifts," about which I will say more in a minute.

Third, the Holy Spirit has "sanctified" me, that is, "made me holy." Oh-oh! one thinks; "I" am not holy, and it'd be false advertising to list me as such. In the Scriptures and Luther's teaching, however, being holy is a gift, a benefit unearned. Being holy means being set apart, which we are.

The Holy Spirit "has kept me in the true faith." This is not to say that no one will ever "fall" from faith, but if one does so, it is not the work or fault of the Holy Spirit. The promise of God is that we will be kept in the true faith.

We connect many other tasks to these. Thus we say that the Holy Spirit "inspires" the sacred Scriptures, so that through them we can be called, enlightened, made holy, and kept in the true faith.

One of the letters of Peter says that "men and women moved by the Holy Spirit spoke from God" (2 Peter 1:21), so we attach the acts of preaching and teaching, conversing and listening, with the Holy Spirit's work.

Luther sometimes called the Holy Spirit *Creator Spiritus*; we believe that the Holy Spirit is creative, having hovered over the waters, as in the creation story in Genesis 1:2.

The Holy Spirit hovers over the waters of baptism, as did the dove of the Holy Spirit at Christ's baptism, and we make the sign of the Holy Spirit on the body of the baptized as a token that that person has been redeemed by Christ.

Only one rule is consistent: the Holy Spirit always works through and is connected with "means," the Word and the sacraments and all their extensions.

We may feel "spiritual" and speak of "winds of the Spirit" in nature; well and good, but this is not what the scriptural Holy Spirit refers to.

38. In What Ways Does the Holy Spirit Work in the Church?

This question can be given a precise Lutheran answer, too. As long as we have the book open, we can turn a few pages further to the Large Catechism, one of whose most beautiful and comforting sections deals with "I believe in the Holy Spirit." It takes up precisely again the point of this question, work "in the church."

Answer: "[The Holy Spirit] first leads us into his holy community, placing us in the church's lap, where he preaches to us and brings us to Christ." Elaboration: "In the first place [again!], [the Holy Spirit] has a unique community in the world, which is the mother that begets and bears every Christian through the Word of God, which the Holy Spirit reveals and proclaims" (Large Catechism, Creeds 37, 42).

I can't resist quoting more: "I believe that there is on earth a holy little flock and community of pure saints under one head, Christ. It is called together by the Holy Spirit in one faith, mind, and understanding. . . . I was brought into it by the Holy Spirit and incorporated into it through the fact that I have heard and still hear God's Word, which is the beginning point for entering it" (Creeds 51–52).

While Lutherans may not and probably should not pick a fight about the phrase, they can feel a bit uneasy with the accent of the common phrase in the question, "Have you found Jesus as your personal Savior?" They may be glad that you have, but the phrase is very individualistic and neglects to witness to how the Holy Spirit works through community. And have I "found" Jesus? Jesus through the Holy Spirit has "found" us. It may be true that one can read a Gideon Bible in a hotel room all alone and be brought to faith. But even the placement of that Bible would not occur did not a community, an agency of Christian community, place it there.

The Holy Spirit usually "calls" through our parents, teachers, pastors, spouse, friends—people important to us. They point us to the Scriptures and the church, where the Holy Spirit has been waiting, is active, and will complete the work—through the church, however broadly or narrowly we define it.

In the Small Catechism we read exactly the same words for life in community as we do in the case of the person: "[The Holy Spirit] calls, gathers, enlightens, and sanctifies the whole Christian church on earth and keeps it united with Jesus Christ in the one true faith."

So if the Holy Spirit always works through "means," so the Holy Spirit also works through the church, and thus through "community."

39. What Do Lutherans Believe about the "Baptism of the Holy Spirit"?

Here Lutherans part company with those Christians who say there are two baptisms, one by water and the other of the Holy Spirit. Such faithful, fervent, and well-intentioned believers see the one baptism as external and the other internal, one as an outer ceremony and the other an experience in the heart and soul.

In Lutheran teaching there is, as the letter to the Ephesians says, "one baptism," just as there is "one Lord, one faith, . . . one God." In that section the accent is on the claim that there are not baptisms of Paul and Apollos and other disciples, just as there are not in our present world baptisms of Lutherans and Catholics and Presbyterians. Yet that one baptism also covers the fact that once it occurs it is complete. The Christian does not lack empowering gifts that come with baptism. (In a later section on baptism I may sound somewhat contradictory and suggest that the baptized Christian is never a finished product, but that theme addresses a different issue than we are dealing with here.

Most Christians who speak of a separate "baptism of the Holy Spirit" connect it with other acts, such as "speaking in tongues," prophesying, healing, and the like. All of these may be legitimate expressions of the life of the baptized, but it is confusing to speak of them as second baptisms that might take away from the fulfilling character of baptism.

The bottom line: in Lutheran understandings of biblical promises and terms, in baptism the Holy Spirit is not holding back, keeping something in reserve, suggesting that something more is necessary and coming. If one should die right after baptism, she will not have lacked any aspect of what God promises through the Holy Spirit, and there is no need to await a second inner baptism or think that one has been cheated because such a baptism has not been sought or realized.

In inter-church relations and in families where the "baptism of the Holy Spirit" is separated from "water baptism," there is no reason to pick a fight. We should be so happy that baptism has occurred and keeps working its effects that we might enjoy the effects rather than argue over them. At the same time, a believer has to be prepared not to feel beat down when someone suggests that she is half-finished just because she does not follow their interpretation and practice.

40. What Do Lutherans Believe about the "Gifts of the Holy Spirit"?

Lutherans ordinarily connect "gifts" of the Holy Spirit with "fruits" or effects of the Holy Spirit's work. On this subject, several New Testament writers such as Paul cannot say enough, can hardly hold themselves in as they run through catalogs on which they hoped congregations of old would reflect and which congregations today read and are to enjoy. So hold on to your seats as this cornucopia of gifts or fruits gets inventoried:

"The fruit of the Spirit is love, joy, peace, patience, kindness, generosity, faithfulness, gentleness, and self control" (Galatians 5:22). By contrast, note what author Paul has just cataloged as life apart from the Spirit—"the works of the flesh": "The works of the flesh are obvious: fornication, impurity, licentiousness, idolatry, sorcery, enmities, strife, jealously, anger, quarrels, dissensions, factions, envy, drunkenness, carousing, and things like these" (5:19–21). The contrast is sufficiently strong to inspire Christians to accept, enjoy, and put to work the fruit of the Spirit.

The other theme that Paul and some other writers stress is that there is only one Holy Spirit and that all the gifts come from this one source. Having said that, everything breaks loose, since these gifts differ and they come to diverse kinds of people with different natural gifts and callings.

What ties them all together is that they are to work for the common good through community, as in the Christian church. The reason for stressing this is to remind ourselves that biblical writers and Lutheran teachers seem very concerned lest the recipients of the gifts forget that they *are* gifts, not achievements, that the receipt of these does not bring with it a certificate licensing "bragging rights" or encouragement to hoard the gifts.

The "gifts of the Spirit" are connected with and issue from God's generosity. It is not imagined that the Holy Spirit will run out of or will withhold whatever is needed for us to fulfill our callings.

There is one twist to this common Christian teaching that Lutherans cherish. It connects "I believe in the Holy Spirit," and in "one holy catholic church, the community of the saints," with "the forgiveness of sins, resurrection of the body, and eternal life." Those three are the sum and substance, the climax, the omega point of all "gifts of the Spirit."

The Large Catechism (Creed 61) summarizes this well: "Creation is now behind us, and redemption has also taken place, but the Holy Spirit continues his work without ceasing until the Last Day, and for this purpose has appointed a community on earth, through which he speaks and does all his work."

41. Is "Speaking in Tongues" a Necessary Sign of the Holy Spirit in One's Life?

No, say Lutherans. But it is an option. A minority of Lutheran congregations belong to what has been called "the charismatic movement," a preferred term within Lutheranism for "Pentecostalism" and its practices. Individual Lutherans may also have sought the experience of "tongues" and will testify that they have received "the gift of tongues." Odds are that newcomers to Lutheranism will travel far before they come to a parish that is part of the movement, yet they should be aware of it.

Lutherans tend to live with or between two attitudes on this subject.

On one side, they are reluctant to rule out something that in the New Testament is mentioned as a gift of the Spirit. In 1 Corinthians 14, Paul sets out to put the practice of "speaking in tongues" in perspective. He is not referring to the special miraculous observance described in the Pentecost story of Acts 2, where visitors from various nations who spoke other languages heard Jewish-speaking disciples speaking in their own languages—even though these disciples could not speak them otherwise. This is called *xenolalia*, speaking in strange languages. Now and then you will hear someone report that English speakers in Toronto, for example, suddenly erupt into intelligible Chinese in praise of the Spirit.

Almost always speaking in tongues refers to a kind of ecstatic speech made up of unintelligible syllables, in which the speakers believe they are experiencing the presence and activity of the Spirit.

On the other hand, some Lutherans measure speaking in tongues as a low-rated gift, as it was by Paul the apostle, who wrote that he would rather speak an intelligible word than many in "tongues." The Lutheran Confessions take up 1 Corinthians in only one context: criticizing Catholics (mainly) who resisted translation from Latin to the languages that people could understand in the Bible and in church. They stressed that all our language should be intelligible. (Let it be confessed that sometimes Lutheran theologians speak in such technical jargon that it sounds like unintelligible, though not ecstatic, speaking in tongues. They *can* translate their difficult terms into simpler ones.)

In the modern church many Lutherans have felt disruption in their congregations where tongues-speakers press their gift on others and, some say, look down on those who do not seek *glossolalia*, the technical term for the practice. One can overhear pastors who are unmoved by tongues, treating it like smallpox: "Has it broken out in your congregation?" It can be divisive.

At best, the practice can serve as a way of experiencing the Holy Spirit, and it can be used to enhance gifts that one already has—before one returns to the quest for worshiping and speaking in clear and intelligible language.

Let it also be noted that the twentieth-century-born Pentecostal movement, now thriving in the new century, is an enormous factor in church growth, especially in the poorer world, and that "Pentecostal Christianity" is a current that runs alongside Catholicism, Orthodoxy, Protestantism, and Evangelicalism, and in some places outpaces them all. So Lutherans who are not moved by "tongues" may well be moved by those who are moved by it.

42. What Is the Holy Spirit's Role in Evangelism?

Answer: In a way, it's the whole deal. The "way" means that the Holy Spirit who always works through "means" always uses people as bearers of the means. Luther and Lutheran theology keep saying, "I am not making this up!" when they tell the Christian story or preach the Word of God. One can sit in a room and feel the stirring of winds of the Spirit, can find the spiritual in art and poetry, and, for that matter, can get spiritual feelings in a warm bath. Well and good, we suppose. But none of them is a part of evangelism.

Evangelism can always and only work when it is connected to the Christian story. It begins by reference to a Creator God, who has made us and our world and gives us the gifts that go with it. The evangelizer asks whether the conversation partner, often a seeker, recognizes this. Both may believe in the Big Bang or Cosmic Ooze or the creativity of Mozart, but Christian evangelism backs up and sees the source and origin of these in God's creation. And there—Aha! and Yeah!—one finds the Creator Spirit active.

Evangelism moves on to see how the Holy Spirit in Scripture tells how God has a special story through a people called Israel, and through the call of its prophets. The prophets of Israel invoke the Spirit, the *ruach,* the wind of God. Their language draws us up short by pointing to our need for a change, a turning, a reversal of our way. With this comes the prophetic word of promise: that the God of Israel elects also to include us in that story. The Holy Spirit seals it.

Evangelism comes to focus in God's work in the evangel, the good news of what God is doing for the other person in Jesus Christ. As the Lutheran catechisms both stress and the Bible makes clear again and again, nothing would happen now to the human heart without divine agency. And that agency, "calling, gathering, enlightening, sanctifying, and keeping" a person, is always described as the work of the Holy Spirit.

Evangelism always calls people to the company of others, to colleagues in seeking, to community, to the communion "of saints." And none of these would exist were it not for the Holy Spirit's work.

Clever people can make arguments for the existence of God. Noisy people can be loud about self-help and moralism. Excited people can jump up and down and advertise various benefits. But only when God is offered, not described; when the benefits of Jesus Christ for the human heart are given, and again not merely described as in a lecture; when the holy community invites, opens its doors, and members make room in their circle and their hearts—only then would we say that the role of the Holy Spirit is recognized and is working its effects.

43. Does the Holy Spirit Work outside the Church?

When speaking of the work of the Holy Spirit, there is a danger that one can limit the understanding of God's doings. Lutherans would divide God's work in two. On the one hand, we see God being active in "creative and ordering" work, and, on the other, we witness God's "saving and redeeming work." From the second aspect, since the Holy Spirit is connected with the gospel of Jesus Christ and the community called the church, the answer to the present question would be no, the Holy Spirit does not work outside the church.

To stop there, however, is to stop way short of what Lutherans picture when they talk of the *Creator Spiritus,* the Creator Spirit. Here there are no limits, since the whole universe, we hear, is upheld by the word of God and that word is effected through the Spirit.

We may speak of good and God-pleasing things going on in the human world, the world of politics and government, of arts and industry, of learning. Here the Lutheran writings relate everything again to the creative power of God. In Isaiah, King Cyrus is called the "anointed," the "shepherd of God's people," even though he does not know God's name (Isaiah 44:28; 45:1). Paul says that government is "ordained of God." Christians are to eat and drink and do "all things" to the glory of God. In Colossians 1:15–20 we read that all things—*all things!*—are created in and through and for Christ, and in him all things hold together. God's rain is to fall on the just and the unjust. The Lutheran Confessions say that even people who adhere to other religions, and thus do not have saving knowledge of God, are gifted with conscience and natural knowledge that helps them serve as citizens. In all these cases, the empowering agent is the Holy Spirit.

So we might say the Holy Spirit has two kinds of workings, but to understand them and to give thanks for them, the Christian has her own insight and spin: the Spirit works through means and visible things and persons, always serving the purposes of God the Holy Trinity, Father, Son, and Spirit.

chapter seven

Salvation

44. How do Lutherans connect "faith" with the "grace" of God?

The grace of God is the generous outpouring of all that is good, all that we need, issued from the very heart of God, with no strings attached. When all human effort has failed to bring assurance this one motion of God remains. And the believer, receiving it in faith, is justified, made right with God. In fact, grace is received by faith *alone*! Paul said it in Romans 3:28 "For we hold that a person is justified by faith *alone* apart from works prescribed by the law."

Oh-oh! Paul did not say exactly that. I cheated in that quotation by inserting the italicized word *alone*. If you noticed that it is not in the original Greek of St. Paul, you are not the first to have done so. The concept associated with the word *alone* scandalized the people in Rome to whom the apostle wrote. The word itself in Luther's translation offended the authorities in Rome who wanted to mix faith with human striving. It also nettles contemporaries— each of us?—when we pursue self-help techniques in efforts to please ourselves and to please God along the way. The temptation remains strong to substitute our "works" for faith *alone*.

Luther and Lutherans are so desperate about getting the point across that they could be accused of overstating the case, if the case could be overstated, and thus of distorting the gospel.

Put another way: Luther was so insistent and exuberant about faith that he cheated a bit in this translation. In our time paraphrases, which are informal renderings of the Greek into English, are so common that readers might hardly notice a word that was inserted in a text to help bring out the point. Luther, however, was so known for insisting on a single word as short as "is" (as when the scripture hears Jesus saying of the bread at the Lord's Supper: "this *is* my body"...), that he should be held to account for inserting the word "alone" after "faith."

Luther, a highly fallible human being, did not put that word "alone" there out of ignorance or to display arrogance. Nor was he as a translator facing a bare cupboard of such texts. They are abundant. Many of the portrayals of God in the Bible show how divine grace is the deepest expression of the love of God and faith is the distinctive way to receive it. Luther seems to have made this ornery move in his translation in order to reinforce what he insisted was the grand theme of the Bible. Call it a paraphrase.

We might wander a bit and let this connection of grace and faith slip from our minds. We might be tempted to compromise or bargain it away. "Good-bye, faith; we have to leave room for a smidgen of counsel to seek God's favor with "faith-*plus*" something or other." However, we might not have caught on in 999 readings, but this thousandth time, almost bludgeoned to attention by the word, we might catch on. Lutherans believe that catching on to *grace* and receiving it in *faith* is a linkage that assures us that we have taken the main point of the gospel to heart and had it etched there.

45. What Does It Mean to Be "Saved"?

L utherans might, but probably don't, run around looking strangers in the eye and asking, "Are you saved?" The accosted person might be tempted to turn around and ask, "Why do you ask?" You wouldn't think of asking me, almost a stranger, how much money I have in the bank or what my sex life is like or if I have anxieties undisclosed to date or other lesser things on my mind. Yet on the biggest, most important, and in some ways most personal but still revealing answer, we might prefer not to hear the question.

Turn it around. We can often take a question and restate it so that it is helpful for explaining features of the faith. Then one can hear the other person not acting as a census taker with numbers in mind to brag or complain about: "Eight out of nine of the players on our team are saved!" "That movie is a good one, because the Christian newspaper tells me that he is saved." Never mind that the film is bad, the story is a mess; all is well because *at least* the producer has good intentions, and doesn't that count for something? Keep the turn-around translation going; maybe the questioner does have my best interests, not his scorecard, on the mind. And that is a loving concern.

So are you "saved"? That question gets interesting only when we know from what, for what, toward what, and by what means we are saved. We can be saved from bankruptcy and bad investing policies, saved from an addiction, saved because we have prayed to have a different status before God than the corrupt and wearying path of least resistance that we have chosen.

To be saved is to be revisited by God even when we do not deserve it. To be saved is to experience God's diagnosis of what is really, really bothering us and to take steps to change that. To be saved is to be rescued out of the evil clutches of bad habits and bad company.

To be saved is to have heard, received, pondered, and entertained a way of life that flows from the story of God's acting spontaneously, not counting the cost of our sins—but still putting us to work in a kind of garden of life. To be saved is to respond to the biblical stories of what Jesus said he did and why he did it: and that doing "it" points immediately and completely to Gods' work under the label "grace."

To be saved is to be appraised by God and found lacking—and then being picked up by God and placed in a new situation. Whatever held me back—"sin, death, the devil, or the self," has lost its hold and I am made free.

To be saved is always connected with the work of Christ, who acquired the name "Savior" because he steps out of his way to make himself available to us, turns to the Father and asks that God will release us from whatever kept us from serving God completely and being free to serve our fellows.

For those who take the long view, to be saved is to be assured that the love of God that rescued us now is not going to desert us, going to deprive us of the fulfillment that comes with all the promises of God. That means that our physical death does not terminate the connection of the flow. Whatever we picture and however we picture it, "to be saved" means to be situated where God's presence will never be revoked and where God's light will shine.

46. Must We Be Baptized in Order to Be Saved?

Yes and no. Yes, because the Scriptures connect being baptized with being saved. Not all Christians make as much of this connection as Lutherans do. Some think that they find us scraping at the edges of the catechetical barrel to come up with appropriate texts. Thus if you are in a Christian tradition that makes less or little of baptism, you might skim the later pages of the New Testament and blink, missing what Luther found for the Small Catechism and what he there made large. It's in the text on "The Sacrament of Holy Baptism," question 3: "How can water do such great things?" Then: "St. Paul writes in Titus 3 [verses 5–8]: 'He saved us . . . in virtue of his own mercy, by the washing of regeneration and renewal in the Holy Spirit."

Question 2 makes the strong point with a strong text: "What benefits does God give in Baptism?" And the answer includes the phrase "In Baptism God . . . gives everlasting salvation to all who believe what he has promised," as Mark 16:16 says, "The one who believes and is baptized will be saved." Then, when comfort is needed, the reader turns to the other half of the line, "But the one who does not believe will be condemned."

I bring up that text and point to it in order to allay anxiety when baptism has been neglected or not possible. Is the unbaptized newborn who experiences SIDS, Sudden Infant Death Syndrome, "unsaved"? Is the catechized adult driving to church for baptism but killed in a car crash "unsaved"?

Because the Scriptures are so serious about connecting baptism with salvation, it is natural that thoughtful people have devoted much energy to answering this question. Some speak of the "baptism of desire." Others cannot picture God penalizing infants of non-believing, half-believing, or casually believing parents for keeping one from being baptized and thus saved.

The whole track of questioning here is a bit off the mark. Lutherans do not usually start or end with little examinations of every molecule of ink in any text that talks about baptism. Instead, they see baptism as an encompassing act, through which we are "named" and "initiated" and "adopted" into the company of Christ, where we receive all the benefits of God.

Baptism is being "buried with him [Christ] by baptism into death, so that just as Christ was raised from the dead by the glory of the Father, so we too might walk in newness of life" (Romans 6:4). It might be better to pose the question in such a way that the answer spells out the benefits of baptism as a means of grace that saves us.

47. Will Non-Christians Be Saved?

Lutherans take seriously the scriptures that attach everything about being saved to the work of God through the Holy Spirit in Christ. They are also serious about the biblical texts that picture what those miss who have never heard of Jesus Christ and had no chance—no chance at all!—to become a Christian. Lutherans share the sense of puzzlement, rage, or at least uneasiness about unanswerable questions such as "How can that be fair?" "We" happen to be born in a place where Christianity is the option for us that Hinduism is for a Hindu child, and Islam is for a Muslim child who will quite likely go through life never meeting a non-Muslim, never being bidden to prayer except to Allah. Is it fair to be beneficiaries of geographical roulette, playing the lottery of picking the right parents?

Here's a Lutheran way of answering this question. God has given and told us all that we need to know to be "saved" and to invite others to be saved. God does *not* answer every question we might have. Here's a bit of a Lutheran shocker, not often discussed: in an argument with Erasmus over the bondage of the will, Luther worked himself into and out of a corner by saying something like this, which for a moment I will take in Latin: God is both *deus absconditus* and *deus revelatus*. In the former case we can see the word "absconded," but here the point is that God is hidden. Then God is also revealed. God is revealed in broad ways in nature, in conscience, and in reason, but in a saving way in Jesus Christ and "the means of grace." Luther says that even when revealed, God remains hidden: who would look for God in the bread and wine of Communion, the water of baptism, smudged ink in a Bible, bad grammar in preaching and teaching? But there God is.

The startling thing confronts his readers when Luther goes on to say that God is hidden not only *in* revelation but *behind* revelation. This is a way of saying that God is God and we are not; the mind of God is other than the human mind; the treasures of wisdom of God are vast, boundless, and ours are small and spare and sparse. We have heard of an exchange at the Second Vatican Council when two cardinals posed the issue of debating a change in Catholic teaching against birth control. One asked, "But if we change, what will happen to all the women we sent to purgatory for violating our teaching?" The other answered with a question, "Are you sure God ratifies all our decisions?"

Our decisions have to be based on the knowledge we have: to share the word of grace, to take the commands of God seriously, to relish and be joyful about the word of salvation that we have received. The rest we leave up to God. In one biblical parable Jesus tells of some workers who knocked themselves out all day but turned themselves and their yield over, saying that they were unprofitable servants, they had done all they could, and now it was up to the master. So with us.

God is a God of love, expansive, boundless love, who does not want any to "perish," to be deprived of the wonders of salvation. That love can win out in the end. *When* we ask questions about that is key. Someone has quoted the legend of Faust, who sold his soul to the devil so he could gain all knowledge. At the end of his life he knew what is in the libraries and encyclopedias, but he saw limits and said, "I now do know that we can nothing know." That same someone went on to say that that humble word may be marvelous for Faust or us at the end of life, but it is a horrible thing to put as a motto under the desk glass of a first-year collegian. We are to respond, evangelize, and hope on the basis of what God has revealed, commanded, and promised. And then we turn over the question about non-Christians being saved to God, who is not limited by our decisions, conclusions, or interpretations.

chapter eight

The Church

48. What Does It Mean to Be a Church "Member"?

All baptized Christians are, of course, members of the Body of Christ, of the one, holy, catholic, and apostolic church—whether they "do" anything about it or not. "Doing" something cannot mean that one merely "signs on" to a local congregation, thus becoming a member of it. Nor can it mean that by letting one's name appear on a congregational "membership list," a person has begun to realize the joys and benefits or, on the other hand, has begun to be responsible. It may be unfortunate that we use the same word for participation in the Christian church or in one of its local congregations *and* for belonging to all other kinds of voluntary associations. Lutherans may encourage their "members" to join and participate in all kinds of service organizations, many of which do God-pleasing work. At the same time, they do not picture that being a member of a Scout troop, a service club, or a political organization is on the same level as church membership. They do not say that in a proud manner, suggesting that they can and do look down their noses at other organizations that have membership lists.

Instead, they do say that the church as the Body of Christ and as a local congregation, an element in that body, implies a relationship that is not bordered by death. Instead, it brings the promise of eternal relations with God in Christ. While it is true that in the modern world, churches tend to advertise their wares, implicitly and often explicitly fish for members, and hope that a prospect "chooses" or "decides" for this particular church in this denomination (there is no way to get away from such impressions), Christians are to consider their participation as a gift, not an achievement. They may know that the choice or decision will depend on all kinds of accidental factors, such as where members live and where their church is located, whom they marry, whether they marry, or what kind of greeting they receive while looking over churches. Their stress is not on their great achievement of finding the right fit, but on the exhilaration they feel when they are connected with a vibrant gathering called a congregation, or on the need they recognize to participate in the never-ending process of reforming such a gathering.

So, however it happens, one "joins" and becomes a "member." This question about what it means to be a church member moves beyond the theology of the church to the practice. One has become a member when baptized as an infant, in cases where one or both parents or caretakers are members and promise to bring up the child in the nurture of a congregation. (One is *not* "baptized Lutheran," or committed to "Old First Church," just because a baptism happened there.) At the time of first communion or the affirming of baptism that is sometimes called "confirmation," it is assumed that the newcomer has been instructed in the faith and in the assumptions of congregational and larger-church life. Usually in a ceremony the new member-to-be or new member is asked whether he or she will be a responsible hearer of the Word and participator at the Lord's Table. The existing congregation welcomes the one who makes the promises. Usually some details of Christian practice then get announced and affirmed.

Some congregations have membership lists or books to sign. Often one becomes a member through a letter of transfer from another congregation that assures the new church home that the one being transferred is an active and responsible Christian in the former community. Those who are realistic are likely to wink and say, "And then they receive 'offering envelopes.'" Without the wink, something is communicated that suggests that membership involves a vocation, a calling, a response to a loving God by bringing gifts for the work of the church and donating hours and prayer time to advance Christ's cause.

In Lutheran theology one never *is* but is always *becoming* a Christian and thus also a member. The church is not made up of human finished products, and membership is just a step along the path of discipleship and growth.

49. Why Is the Church So Full of "Sinners"?

After two thousand years of church life, there are good reasons for Christian church members to be taken aback when many in the public are surprised to find sinners in the church. They have to show a bit of patience when someone dismisses the church with the word that hypocrites and other sinners are there. Of course sinners are there. If there were not, there would be no church members. There is no place for those who would recruit the sinless to invite people to take part, and there is no place either for those who think that taking the beginning steps of the Christian walk in the church community means perfection. From every Lutheran pulpit one should hear only the message that listeners should confront themselves and discern the ways they offend God and hurt others so that they can then receive with joy the good news that God has accepted them because of the self-giving activity of Jesus Christ. Every Lutheran message, whether in classes or sanctuaries, clearly presupposes that sinners are there, that 100 percent of those in range need to be addressed as sinners.

That does not mean that such pulpits and congregations transact with a "hell fire and damnation" message. Those who study the gospel and know anything about psychology or rhetoric, the art of persuasion, know that there are other ways than the hell fire and damnation approach to help induce people to bring their woes and cares, their disappointments and shortcomings, and most of all—no use mincing words—their sin before God. The point of messages that begin with diagnosis and follow up with God's good news is that God does not leave or want to leave the sinner bound in sin or immersed in the task of accounting for all the sins one can think of. No, the word of the gospel is waiting. Lutherans like to take a biblical concept and talk about "growth in grace." Why grow, if from day one there is no more need for grace?

Having said all that, it is important also to affirm the obvious: on the church rolls and in the pews and aisles, along with forgiven people who show that they are growing in grace, there are also scoundrels, laggards, the self-deceived, those "curved in upon themselves," who are a poor advertisement for the life in Christ. Better that they manifest what the early Christian communities did when outsiders who observed them had to say, "See how they love one another!" Better that those not yet in the circle of God's love and community also say, "See how they love everyone!" Most Lutheran classes and sermons offer people help with diagnosing their sins and shortcomings. They attempt to help strugglers, addicts, secret sinners, and gross ones alike to examine themselves, to try to discern why they fall short, and then to show them where to go for a changed Christian life.

The apostle Paul, who so strongly influenced this church, was a self-reflective person, who used himself as an example: he wanted to be good and to do good, but something in him—world? devil? flesh? weakness? temptation? self-delusion?—kept him from taking the turn or staying on the proper path. He had to call for divine aid. He in effect taught believers that they should not claim blamelessness but rather should beckon people to take part with them in the daily acts of renewal that get fulfilled in lives with rich vocations and demonstrated works of love.

An old and maybe overworked observation had it that just as Noah preferred the stench within the ark to the storm outside it, so Christians in community have to know that they not only inhale the stench but contribute to it in the ark or, in this metaphor, the church. But they consider the alternative. While there are plenty of good people in the storm out there, those in the ark, the sanctuary, the church, get to find the resources for dealing with their limits and the world's often-wrong attractions.

Every reformer weeps to see the churches torn apart by sinful troublemakers, looked down on when public sinners get exposed, and demonstrably full of fakes and the fallen. Every reformer is unhappy when this has to be pointed out to a questioner who asks, "Why is the church full of 'sinners'?" Every grieving reformer looks into the mirror before looking out the window and sees that the chief place to meet sinners is in that looking glass. Yet the informed person who recognizes this is not a participant in a Greek tragedy but a joyful respondent to God's redeeming claims and the guiding hand of Christ as one walks, lifelong, on a pilgrimage path—with other sinners.

50. What Do We Mean by the "Visible" and the "Invisible" Church?

The terms "visible" and "invisible" connected with "church" are not directly and exactly traceable to biblical bases, but they can perhaps be inferred from passages of Scripture. These terms are of limited usefulness, but they suggest some realities with which Christians have to deal. Someone once said that the handy thing about the idea of the invisible church is that in it one can display invisible love. It is possible to use the notion of the invisible church as a way of lessening the pressure on what came to be called the "visible church" to live up to anything connected with God's calling.

The church is always made up of people. Let me say it again: unless one is speaking about people, one cannot be speaking about the church. The classic Lutheran writings, as we have already noted, insist that the church is not a philosophical idea. It is not a notion in the mind of God. It is not something that philosophers inspired by Plato would exhaust by speaking of "ideas."

The church is people. And people are always visible. True, people who have died in faith and gone before may belong to what many believers like to call "the church triumphant." On All Saints Day and all other times when Christians gather, they keep in mind the people, the members, who are participating in "eternal life." But here on earth, church = people. And people are visible. When they have talked about the invisible church, thinkers from Augustine in the fifth century down through John Calvin in the sixteenth and many others, including many Lutherans in the twenty-first, are really pointing to the fact that no one except God can know the boundaries of the church, how far they extend, and whom they include.

Most who use the term "visible church" suggest that there are boundaries and that these include and enclose those who are members of the church, who make a confession of faith, who appear "on the church rolls," who engage in events that lead historians to talk about responsible church life and corrupt and self-defeating church life. One good thing about Luther's kind of accents on the visible and invisible church is that those who voice them leave room for the understanding that not all who are part of God's flock are members of particular congregations or church bodies, and they might not even be able to be found and identified at all. While reforming the Roman Catholic church of which he was a part, Luther always had to make clear that through all the ages there were countless disciples, followers of Christ, even if they were not within boundaries that were acceptable on biblical grounds.

Being part of the visible church commits its members to making the works of love visible, reforming the groups who make up church on any terms. It is a relief to many Christians to be reminded that God knows those who are God's; that we do not have to judge who is "in" and who is "out." The task instead is to work with those who are visible members of visible bodies, to show charity to those who may be in God's flock but are not "registered" to their satisfaction, and, even more, to let Christ's love spill out from them to everyone. When this love is put into action, there is no room for the label "Members Only," but there is always the invitation "Y'all come," become "visible."

51. What Is the Priesthood of All Believers?

You can go through life and not hear or need to use the term "the priesthood of all believers." Most members of most Lutheran churches might recognize it in two cases. One, when there is an argument about the status of clergy and laity—and Lutherans cannot always avoid such argument. The other use is more positive and handier; when Christians of persuasions like the Lutheran are looking for a term that works to minimize the distinction between clergy and laity or especially when they want to show how powerful the role of laypeople is conceived to be and can be, they reach into history and often come up with "the priesthood of all believers."

To see why the term is of at least limited use, note that in the previous paragraph the term "laity" shows up twice and "lay" is there once, though I have some hesitation in using these terms. This is not because "lay" and "laity" are not noble, dignified, and historically rich terms, but because, in the modern world, "lay" has often come to be equated with "amateur." Sometimes people use the word in an effort to show that they are humble or not fully informed, as in "Of course, I am just a layperson, and the laity is not expected to . . ." It may be that some self-defensive clergy talk behind the backs of some members and dismiss them as uninformed. None of these usages does justice to the biblical concepts designating those who are not in what Martin Luther would call "the office" of professional clergy.

Another problem with the still-valuable term is that the word "priest" is fairly rare among Lutherans and other Protestants. People associate it with Eastern Orthodox or Roman Catholic church life. So to speak of "the priesthood of all believers" demands several acts of translation. In recent decades Lutherans, Episcopalians, and others have tried to clear out cobwebs and clutter and find a term that communicates instantly. They are converging on "the ministry of the baptized." That does not solve everything, because one must still define "ministry" and find terms that point to what the professionals in the office of ministry are defined as doing or intending to do.

In world religions and in much of Christianity, the priest was both a human means of accessing God and a human means of blocking the way to God. In the long history of the term, it often referred to elite groups who would bring an offering, perhaps of plants but more often of animals, to represent the sacrifice of the people, who were not supposed to do the sacrificing themselves. In Catholicism and some other Christian contexts, the priest is unique. If one could not work through the officially ordained priest, ordained under the right auspices, the sacraments were not valid.

At the Second Vatican Council, in language advocating reform, there was a stress on the high value of the laity. Laypeople could go where priests were not welcome or were too visible. The laity outnumbered the clergy many times over, and they should be honored for their calling.

It is true that Martin Luther did speak of "the priesthood of all believers." There was, after all, a verse in a New Testament letter in which the writer said that the recipients were "a royal priesthood" (1 Peter 2:9). One of the strongest accents in Luther's understanding is that the priesthood of all believers meant that all could represent the people to God. Christians could forgive each other, not making them "do penance" to pay for their sins, but asking them to serve others. The easiest way to condense this is to say that all Christians could pray intercessory prayers. The term was not designed to show who did *not* have clergy privileges, who was a half-finished Christian.

Inevitably, in a world of specialization, the priest, now usually the pastor, took on specialized roles. He—and most of the while it has been "he"—did the preaching, confessing, and administering in a congregation. Yet as laypeople around the Christian world more often than before enjoyed higher education and acquired all kinds of technical skills, it was important to look for a term that was not so limiting. "The ministry of the baptized" is coming to be!

In most Lutheran bodies there is regard for the office of ministry, so they establish ways to differentiate the duties. Some of these go back to the New Testament and the earliest Christian writings that are not in the Bible. In modern Lutheranism one will read that a layperson should not administer the Lord's Supper (Eucharist) and should baptize only in emergency, but the custodianship of these sacred acts is ordinarily in the hands of trained and authorized holders of office.

The phrase "the ministry of the baptized" is designed to enhance the role and image of those who do not hold office, far beyond the duties and privileges connected with the term "priesthood." Lutherans encourage *all* their baptized members to conceive of themselves as agents, representatives, and ambassadors of God.

52. Why Do Lutheran Churches Put Such a Stress on Christian Education?

The question is very much in place. Lutherans *do* put great stress on Christian education. Whether they always live up to their ideals and intentions is another question. Some polls taken in the United States suggest that in many places Lutherans lag behind various kinds of Protestants when it comes to frequency of participation in adult Christian education. Southern Baptists and many sorts of evangelicals tend to do better, even if what many of them do strike Lutherans as being a bit narrow in indoctrination. Rather than judge them, however, Lutherans are exploring their own practices and trying to improve participation.

That they *do* put stress on education and advertise themselves as doing so is or should be instinctual, part of their heritage. After all, or should we say "before all," the Lutheran movement was born in the university. Luther himself was shaped at Erfurt, a university town, and some (as noted in chapter 1, question 1, above) have described the Reformation as a revolt of the junior faculty at Wittenberg. Lutherans played prominent roles in establishing or transforming universities in northern and central Europe, and immigrant Lutherans set up colleges and universities in North America, some forty of which survive and thrive. Similarly, Lutherans are seminary-minded and pay considerable attention to them. History, however, is as history does: many church bodies *had* higher educational ties but let them slip away from their affiliation with the church.

Look up Lutheran congregations almost anywhere and you will find in their bulletins, newsletters, and annual reports reference to nursery schools, preschools, Sunday schools, and, in many cases, parochial schools. Not all of these serve well as instruments for transmitting details of the Bible or history or doctrine. Yet they can serve to help stimulate the imaginations of the young and give them a repertory of stories and themes on which to trade as they grow older.

There is Christian education for the very young as they learn the meaning of their baptism and prepare to reaffirm it as they approach the Lord's Table. "Confirmation instruction" is one term for what happens at that time, and it is intended to be rather intense, just as it is for adult prospects and those being prepared for being confirmed. The great dream in all the congregations is that more and more adults will take seriously the opportunities for Christian education.

Back to the "why" question. The answer is not, "Because one needs to know a few hundred Bible texts and a couple score catechism teachings to be received into the kingdom." Lutherans prize the intellect, but their faith is not intellectualistic; one is not saved by knowledge of "what." They might say, "It is not what you know but whom you know," the living God, the Jesus of history and living faith. Getting to know God and God in Christ through the Holy Spirit is enhanced, however, as one grows in familiarity with what the Bible teaches, what Christian history illustrates, and more. Christianity, also and especially in its Lutheran form, deals with a story, with stories, and these have to be told and taught.

Further, Lutherans encourage growth in faith through encounters with ethics, the sciences, the culture surrounding the church, the markets, politics, and more. They may not take positions on everything that comes up in such realms, but they try to help each other find tools for making decisions. Since the reaches of the faith are numberless, Lutherans encourage people of all ages, into their senior years, to continue to probe texts, ask questions, seek answers, build each other up, and enjoy the excitement of relating the ways and words of God to the world of God's creation.

53. What Is the "Mission" of the Church?

The "mission" of the church is to be "sent out" to *be* and *become* God's presence in the worlds with which its people come into contact. This activity will normally reflect the words and works of Jesus, who called his disciples and followers to do "greater works" than they had seen when he was among them (John 14:12). It is important to remember that "mission" relates to sending and being sent. The church is never church if it only leans back, is static, and complacently lets the world go by. This does not mean that all its activities have to show restlessness or all its members have to be frantic. "Be still and know that God is God" is a biblical mandate (see Psalm 46:10), and it licenses meditation, contemplation, and receiving as part of the mission. Yet normally to speak of mission is to speak of agency, of thinking and doing. While we are thinking of the background of words, it is to be noted that "promise," Luther's favorite word for "the gospel," has "mission" in it: *pro + missio*. The church is sent forth, and God goes before.

Lutherans join other Christians in responding to the word of Jesus at the end of Matthew's Gospel, where he sends them forth "to all nations," and to all the Gospel references to the task of healing, calling people to repentance, working for justice, showing compassion to the stranger and others in need, giving witness to the hope that is in them.

Most Lutherans will tell you that the mission of the church, way down deep, is to address the hungry heart, to convince people of their sin and need for God, to bring about conversion and repentance, to announce the good news, and to celebrate the visible ways God meets people in baptism, the Lord's Supper, and the works of love.

"Way down deep" is not the only direction to go in carrying out the mission of the church. Jesus is quoted as saying that humans do not live by bread alone—but they *do* live by bread. Lutheran Christians who do not respond to human need and who let people starve have not served them. So the mission of the church involves doing justice, loving mercy, and walking humbly with God (see Micah 6:8). It is to share bread with the hungry, clothes for the naked, freedom for the imprisoned. It is to do what the situation demands, keeping the needs of the other person always in view.

We are not talking here just about what an individual receives through the mission of the church, or sets out to achieve as an agent of such a mission. The question is "What is the 'mission' of the church?" Something social, collective, communal, and bonding is going on here. Far more happens when people with informed consciences speak out together and work together, joining forces. It is the mission of the church to support such through prayer and planning and funding. The late Lutheran theologian Joseph Sittler once said that "to be a Christian is to accept what God gives in Christ." Such receiving is the "mission" of the church. But Sittler never pictured that as being passive, since "accepting what God gives" meant accepting agenda, goals, and means of empowerment.

We might do better in the human world to ask, "What is *not* the 'mission' of the church?" If all things are created in and through and for Christ and in him all things hold together, those "all things" are given by God and are to be used in the mission of the church.

54. What Should Be the Church's Relation to Culture?

In simplest terms we might say that culture is anything humans do to nature. A river flows whether noticed or not. Then come photographers and poets and they "do something" with it, contributing to artistic culture. Someone wants to capture its power, so engineers build dams and waterways, and soon an engineering and power culture emerge. Those who live along the river argue about diversion, so a political culture develops.

Christians have no choice but to relate to culture, to see themselves and their church in it, partly as a product of it, often as an agent to do something with it. Humans are to culture as fish are to water. Someone has said that, whoever named the water, it wasn't the fish. They were in it, too close to it. So with cultures; we often notice only the strangers' culture.

Monks who went out to the desert thought they were escaping culture, whereas, as we all know, they were establishing monastic culture and ways of being pious and prayerful. Hermits and recluses try to leave culture behind, and we instead find them living in hermit cultures. On the other extreme, some Christians embrace the surrounding culture so unrestrainedly and emphatically that the culture "takes over," leaving their church to be little more than an advertising or public relations culture.

What should be the relation of the church to culture? There can be no one answer. Certainly, facing Nazi or Maoist cultures is very different from facing pro-religious cultures: the former demands resistance; the latter needs critical support. Theologian H. Richard Niebuhr once worked out a typology of the different ways in which Christians (in his formula, "Christ") relate to culture: Some see Christ *against* culture, an important stance when culture is too alluring and seductive or evil as such. It would have been great had Christians in Germany rebelled against Nazi culture. At the other end are those whose relation was "Christ *of* culture," in which Christians let the culture take over and bless whatever the church finds attractive. Still others said it was Christ *above* culture, urging that Christ or the church is too holy to get into the muck of cultural change.

Lutherans, when they are serious about their heritage, draw on two other models. One is Christ *transforming* culture, in which Christians, often progressives, set their mind on changing the culture, root and branch, and then helping it serve the purposes of God. Many Christian attempts to affect the political order are of this character. Christians in this mode like to talk about progress, about "bringing in the kingdom." Lutherans are not averse to seeing Christ "transform culture," as their participants in arts such as music demonstrate. But they are more at home with the fifth model, "Christ and culture in paradox." That takes a bit of explaining.

Lutherans are to serve in the world and seek its betterment, even though they know that progress and fulfillment will be limited because of human sin, because sin is part of the structures of culture. Thus politics, a noble world that can serve humans by minimizing the violence that is native to history and summoning the energies of people who seek common good, has another side. It also gives expression to self-interest of sorts that often limits the interests and reach of others. Lutherans may have a paradoxical view of the market and commerce. On the one hand, markets can serve divine purposes if and insofar as they contribute to human good, to providing resources. At the same time, built into market life is competition, which is usually fulfilled in limiting the fulfillment of "the other," the competitor. And fulfillment can also mean so much devotion to mammon, Jesus' word for a kind of god of money (see Matthew 6:24), that it takes over mastery at the expense of Christ.

Some Lutherans like to take up old themes, such as "being *in* the world but not *of* it" or others that see the faith, or Christians, or the church, as a kind of "soul" in the body of human works. In any case, culture dare never take over and crowd Christ out. Whatever humans do—and one does not have to be a grump to say this—will be colored by self, self-interest, and probably pride. That is the gloomy side of Lutheran witness about culture. At the same time Lutherans like to quote the biblical themes that stress that whatever one eats or drinks, it is to be done to the glory of God. And that is being faithful in culture.

chapter nine

Worship

55. Why Should We Worship?

The Christian faith is God-centered, and the Lutheran emphasis is to be especially God-centered among all the God-centered movements within the Christian church. Using the word "God-centered" three times, now four times, in as many lines is a device to stress something that is so often forgotten when believers talk about worship. Some talk about worship begins with market analysis: what do people, when polled, say that they want in religious fellowships? If they say they want good educational facilities for children, accessible parking lots, warm greetings at the door, a pastor with personality, and a good gymnasium, the poll takers advise, give them that! It is true that Christians may want the facilities, parking, greetings, and gymnasium and are also God-centered, but we do well to begin at the other end, with God.

There are many ways to do God-centered things, such as when in Christ's name believers feed the hungry or educate children. At root, however, the test of whether God is central in the life of the whole Christian church on earth, in each confessional movement or denomination, and in any particular local church is to see how much emphasis there is on worship. I can be abrupt: we worship because God asks to be worshiped. It is possible to read that sentence and the many passages in Scripture that call for prayer and praise and think that it only reinforces an image of a God who has a strong ego that needs to be fed all the time, on the model of some humans who want to be adored and will remind you every five minutes that you should adore.

In the biblical and Christian case, however, while anthropomorphic thinking, which means imagining God on a human model, is almost inevitable, the ego-seeking dimension of human experience does not reach the reality of God. God, we hear so often and experience so regularly, is love, and love does not seek its own. For God to call to be worshiped is not a divine ego trip but somehow an expression of the love of God, which also means that worship is good for human creatures, the result of God's activities. Rather than prescribe what God should be like, Christians do well to begin, using a phrase of Philip S. Watson's classic book title, with the response "Let God Be God." Letting God be God is responding to God's call to worship God.

We cannot let the discussion end there. The revealed God of Christian faith is never seen in isolation. God creates, someone has said, in order to have company. God being love and acting in love desires what is best for creatures. Here is where the human becomes involved in talk of worship: God's love is provident and all-encompassing; it reaches out to all. So the call to worship must mean—does mean—that the act of worship is also part of human fulfillment. We can speak of worship as fulfilling a need in our nature. Whether or not we believe that humans are "wired for God," that their brains are manufactured in such a way that they cannot leave God-questions out of their minds, it is apparent that humans so regularly seek meaning, find it in God or something else, and are called to do something about it. Martin Luther said that the human has *entweder Gott oder Abgott*. Pardon that intrusion of German; it best suggests what is at stake: the human has "either God or non-God," an idol, a creation. Worshiping God fills in the blank in the human brain in an utterly positive way.

Worship, turning to God in thought and voice, if it is serious and in the biblical tradition, begins with a sense of awe. People need to prostrate themselves before someone or something. They can do it with their eye on the mirror and worship themselves. They may adore things, without reservation. They can turn to the Other, a sort of name for God in this case, and be fearful, because that Other can be tyrannous, as some language of worship might suggest. The God of love, the God who *is* love, however, is not tyrannous but, in the biblical portrayals, is nurturing, responsive, and eager for interaction or conversation. That conversation implies that God not only evokes awe in worship but also is intimate, a still small voice or a voice that welcomes silence: "Be still, and know that I am God!" (Psalm 46:10).

God in biblical portrayals and in human experience is worshiped not only by a solitary person enclosed in a room but in congregation, communion, assembly, where people assume common postures ("Let us bow our heads for prayer," or "Kneel, if you are able," or "Fold your hands") and common words and song. When he dedicated the first church that was not a takeover of an older Catholic church but was a new evangelical creation, the castle at Torgau, Luther said that nothing should ever happen there but that our dear Lord speaks through his holy Word and that we respond in prayer and praise. That's the focus and locale of community worship. Worship allows us to clear our minds of distractions, to concentrate on the biblical story about the acts of God, who calls us to worship. It includes prayer for others.

56. Why Does the Prayer of Confession List Sins I Never Commit?

It may not. It is possible to pray a prayer of confession so inclusive, broad, and sweepingly generic that it never gets specific. Lutherans often pray thus and have no problem with others who pray thus all the time. Some of the prayers of confession used in Lutheran orders of worship, and others that are prepared for specific occasions, as in wartime or hard times or holidays, may include catalogs of sins. It is hard to go down any such list and find that everything being confessed is a match for my way of life in the past week. Not that one is not capable of doing the worst, but it seems dishonest to confess the worst when one's sinning seems middle-sized, cut to the shape of one's own personality and the range of temptations available.

The whole congregation prays all this together, including that list that helps call for self-examination and is designed to prompt resolve not to fall into such sins in the next day or week. Doing so is not a hypocritical act. If I pray that I be forgiven the mistreatment of those "under me" in the office or classroom or family, and there is no one "under me," do I have to fake it? Not at all. Such a register can serve as a reminder of the human condition. It allows me to do some stream-of-consciousness thinking—and, admit it, even in a two-minute prayer of confession the mind is likely to wander off from talking about sins in general to "that reminds me" lists of my own.

There are other and perhaps better reasons to confess with a broad range of sins in mind. I mentioned being linked to broader humanity. Praying thus helps call to mind sins of rich against poor and vice versa; of men and women against each other; of old versus young; of exploiter and exploited. It breeds sympathy for others who "fall into sin" when we remind ourselves how precarious our hold on virtue and the good may be. And prayers of confession can show how connected we are to evils and wrongs everywhere. We may confess that we have misused the resources of the earth, having huge polluters in mind, but as we do so we can rethink our link, our complicity. We do this not to mope or grope for a trophy as Confessor Number One each week, but simply to be realistic and imaginative. Finally, such prayer of confession can be "intercession" for others, our fellow humans who may be guilty of all kinds of evils but will not confess and repent. Here we identify with them.

Now we will change the context a bit and speak of confession not in communal worship but as a personal act. In the Small Catechism Luther asks, "What sins should we confess?" The answer is, "Before God we should confess that we are guilty of all sins, even those which are not known to us," but, before a pastoral confessor, "we should confess only those sins which trouble us in heart and mind." His list is alarming and charming at once: "We can examine our everyday life according to the Ten Commandments—for example, how we act toward father or mother, son or daughter, husband or wife, or toward people with whom we work. . . . We may ask ourselves whether we have been disobedient or unfaithful, bad-tempered or dishonest, or whether we have hurt anyone by word or deed." That does it. That inventory is not a bad list to have in mind in the minutes before a church service begins, as preparation for the more general act of confession.

57. What Is the Function of the Furniture I Might Expect to See in a Lutheran Church?

The question is well put, since most of what one sees is functional, not prescribed in the Bible or historic Lutheran teaching. More likely than not, there will be pews whose function is to seat the congregation. We begin with that rather trivial answer to make the point that the house of God has many simply practical features. By the way, many Lutherans are uneasy with the pew, a rather modern invention. Early Christian worship used house furniture, because the Christians met in houses. Later, through the ages of cathedrals and chapels, movable chairs became common, since congregations had many different uses and foci and could push chairs around. Through the same ages and down into our own time in Eastern Orthodoxy, there may be no seating at all.

The pulpit and/or the lectern are functional. Many Lutheran churches place the pulpit high or render it ornate to give accent to the primacy of the Word of God preached there, but it can also be as simple as a music stand, designed to hold books and notes, lamps and timers. The trend in our time is to make such a stand modest and to allow for the preacher to move around some, to make contact with the congregation. The similarly prime object, accenting the similarly prime focus of worship, is the altar or the table. Historic Lutheran churches tended to place the altar against the wall, at a time when ministers turned their back on congregations when addressing God in the name of the congregation. New or remodeled Lutheran churches, like Catholic churches after the Second Vatican Council (1962–1965), have pulled the altar from the wall and made it appear to be a table, which it may in fact be. This allows for the minister of the sacraments to face the congregation as a gathered community. Such a table is also likely to be large, prominent, perhaps carved with symbols and covered in part with hangings appropriate to the changing times in the church year.

The baptismal font in older churches tends to be a bowl atop or inside a stand, again ordinarily carved and decorated with symbols, signaling how important baptism in public worship is. More recently arranged Lutheran churches will place the font somewhere near where there is access to the sanctuary, symbolic of the way baptism serves as entrance to Christian life. In many Lutheran churches there will be water in the font—not "holy water" or unholy water, but simple water, as was used at baptism. And some Christians will dip fingers into the water and make the sign of the cross, thus identifying with their baptism. Such an act fits the general trend of seeing the congregation not as passive pew-sitters, but as responsive Christians who move and gesture.

58. Why Don't Lutheran Churches Have Altar Calls?

That question would not have been comprehensible in the churches in Europe that serve as grandparents to so many Lutherans in America. In North America, however, the question sometimes comes up because of the presence of so many kinds of evangelicals and Baptists who are seen on television or are part of in-laws' worship or the worship patterns of many who become Lutherans out of such evangelical traditions. "Cradle" Lutherans, whose American Lutheran great-grandparents have never heard of an altar call, might think that here I am uselessly answering an unasked question. To make it useful: the revivalists were seeking converts, enrolling new members, and recalling stories in the book of Acts wherein new converts in effect "came forward" to declare themselves and to be baptized.

It may be that Lutherans, so timid about calling for converts, so shy about stepping forward, might take lessons from the altar-call people. Yet they believe they have such a call "covered" by the whole theme of every act of worship: Lutherans are likely to combine those who have responded to the call with those who may be moved to respond and will be invited to do so in the presence of evangelism committees where "the ministry of the baptized" goes on, or in consultation with the pastor. In a sense, every Lutheran message and set of prayers is an altar call, responded to by people who will find other ways than coming forward to indicate that they want to be called anew to life in Christ. Lutheran preaching is also designed to build up faith already present, to nurture the weak and spiritually hungry, but not always to start from scratch.

59. What Is Preaching, and Why Is It Important?

L utherans so take for granted the importance and centrality of preaching and hearing the word that they may be startled to think that they should think about it. The act of preaching is specifically stressed by Jesus in the Gospels and also by Paul in his letters. Faith comes by hearing, and hearing comes by the word of God (Romans 10:17). Jesus sent out messengers to preach. The Lutheran reformation was fostered by a fresh kind of preaching that focused on attention to the law of God, which was designed to accuse the smug congregations—and in Luther's view we are all smugly "curved in" on ourselves—and then the gospel of God, the good news of what God does in Jesus Christ. Every act of preaching is based on biblical texts; if Lutheran speakers are doing something topical—for example, reviewing Christian teaching—they will ground this in the Bible. Ordinarily they will take off from a "lectionary" text, selected from the Bible in a three-year cycle. This is done in order to help each congregation identify with and be in sympathy with others around the world who are devoting themselves to the same text and theme and to discourage preachers from riding hobby horses or in other ways charging off in all directions, such as in book-reviewing or giving advice for positive thinking in sermons.

Still, the act of preaching is strange, especially in a world where so many make connections via computer or as passive audiences of media or as readers. It is strange because it asks a very frail and fallible person to get up and serve as a human mediator of the divine word. Preaching is designed not to describe God and the ways of God, but to "offer" God in a kind of "sacrament of sound waves." Luther, whose devotion to the printed page of Scripture was second to no one else's, always made clear that priority should be given to the word spoken, designed to reach hearts. Preachers may sometimes use bad grammar, stumble, fail to do their research and preparation as conscience and obligation compel preachers to do. They may offer some chancy opinions on the world around them. They will never live up to the potential of the biblical texts that empower and liberate them. Giving their best, however, they are doing what they are trained and commissioned to do: spreading the Word. And congregants on the listening end are to put to work what they have heard, testing it, critiquing it, enjoying it, and reinforcing it.

60. Why Do Lutherans Insist That Sacraments Be Celebrated Only in Worship Services?

Maybe "insist" is a slightly too strong word, but it does reinforce the theme that sacraments belong to the public service of God. Baptism is to involve more than a baptizer, two parents if there are two, and one child if there is one, just as adult baptism is a public confession before a congregation. The Lord's Supper, Holy Communion, or the Eucharist recalls the collection of disciples at the first event and stresses communion, something that can only be imagined by isolated Christians.

Once that is clear, Lutherans will bring in apparent exceptions. Chaplains sometimes baptize and give bread and wine as Christ's body and blood on battlefields, where nothing else is present except enemy fire. Pastors and chaplains commune individuals who are artificially separated from the worshiping congregation by their illness. When these private acts occur, they can sometimes happen with nothing more said than a formula from Scripture for baptism or for the consecration of bread and wine. These, however, are rare circumstances, and most of the 1.6 billion Christians are to be gathered in campus chapels, little churches at senior citizen homes, and the like. Gathering means the likelihood that preaching will go on, and Lutherans see Word and sacrament as bonded.

61. What Is the Relation between Worship and the Rest of Life?

In many ways worship, properly achieved, *is* the rest of life. That is, at its best, worship is to encompass thinking, acting, believing, and doing. And "the rest of life," whether in marketplace or school setting, legislatures or liveries, is to be worship. Still, we know that most worship occurs at specified times, such as Saturday evening and Sundays, evenings of feast days, and the like. Someone unlocks a door, turns on lights and sound systems, sets out offering plates so the congregation can respond with material blessings in mind and hand, calls in a liturgist and a preacher, and spends an hour worshiping. Then the congregation leaves, going out into the sun of Sunday noon or the dark after vespers.

In the worship service special meanings are given to particular stories. Certain languages develop and are privileged.

One often worships in the company of others who are neighbors, strangers, or friends. Those who offer the Word in messages have to take care not to assume too much in language: who knows, for example, what "propitiation" means? Outside the door MTV and CNN, Disney and Wall Street, "the boss" and the other employees, the good and the evil in bewildering mixture, clueless neighbors and neighbors who come as servants of God, form a jumble.

What are post-worshipers to do in that setting? They are to "be" the church, "doing what the situation demands," as the good Samaritan did. They are to inspire neighbors' comment, "See how they love one another." They are to forgive as they have been forgiven, to be stewards of their possessions on Tuesday and not just some November Sunday at 11:00 A.M. They are to lead transformed lives, exemplifying what early churches did, according to the book of Acts: serving God and others "with glad and generous hearts." They are to seek to change the world, and will do so, whether or not they had planned to or whether or not they interpret their ordinary lives as extraordinarily destined for the kingdom.

chapter ten

The Sacraments

62. Why Do Lutherans Have Two Sacraments?

This question comes up because many Christians, among them Roman Catholics and the Eastern Orthodox, celebrate more sacraments, in most cases seven. Since Lutherans tend to live down the block from or under the same roof with Catholics—there has been much intermarrying—they hear of rites that these other Christians observe but that Lutherans, whether they share the rites or not, do not consider sacraments. Among these are confirmation, marriage, ordination, and the like. Once upon a time this "numbers game"—two sacraments versus seven—inspired heated arguments, and some of the things both parties fought about had some point. As time has passed and conferences have been held, the temperature has gone down, and better questions have come to the fore.

One way to begin to respond to this question about two sacraments—Holy Baptism and the Lord's Supper (or Holy Communion or the Eucharist)—is to pose another question: "Why do Lutherans have sacraments at all?" The first and easiest answer and one that could be decisive is that they have sacraments because Jesus Christ commanded them. He told his disciples that they should go and baptize, making disciples of all nations. The Gospels also report that Jesus commanded the disciples to "do this," namely, eat the bread that was his body and drink the wine that was his blood, in remembrance of him. Jesus recommended or commanded some ceremonies, such as washing each other's feet, but he made clear that doing so was more to follow his example of being humble. In the case of baptism and the Lord's Supper, his command was associated with promise.

Whoever believes and is baptized has eternal life and all the gifts that go with that prospect. Whoever eats and drinks at the Holy Communion table is to receive forgiveness of sins. The fact that such promises come with these two acts is what leads Lutherans to join many other Christians in calling them sacraments and using their distinguishing marks to name them sacraments.

"Distinguishing marks"—there's another feature that goes into defining sacraments. In this case, Christians who live sacramental lives all agree that there are visible signs. These are sometimes called "the elements." Their very physicality helps remind Christians that their faith is very much bound up with the material world, the world we see and touch and feel. One Anglican thinker with a bit of wit, arguing against those who think that Christianity should be "spiritual" and almost "immaterial," said that Christianity is a most material religion: you cannot even get it started without a loaf of bread, a bottle of wine, and a river.

Munching on bread and sipping wine, which is something Christians might do at home or at church outside the sanctuary, is not sacramental. It can be a sign of good fellowship and it certainly provides sustenance for the body. In most ways, however, its benefits are no different from what one might get at a sorority dinner or a club banquet. Bread and wine there are "elements," but for them to be sacramental, Christians who reflect on this have always said something like this: "The Word of God comes to the element and makes of it a sacrament." Now we have another feature of a sacrament. Word + element is the key combination. This the believers receive in faith when the congregation gathers and the words of Jesus' institution at his last supper are repeated as a call for faith and obedience. Grace is central to the promise and, Christians testify, its fulfillment.

Looking back, it is necessary first to remember that the Bible, the only source and norm of faith, does not even come close to using the word "sacrament." It does not spell out what all goes or should go into the definition of a sacrament. It only talks about water connected with God's Word and bread and wine connected with God's Word, and does not set about saying, "Do these two things and call them something special." There was no category, no box, labeled "Sacrament" that says "Fill this in with two rites that you can file here." It does make clear that these rites or practices have to have been initiated by Jesus. The church cannot make them up, label them, and expect them to be categorized with the sacraments.

63. Why Are Sacraments Important?

Sacraments are unimportant outside the faith community. One could say that to the bread maker or the wine producer they are important as factors in the economy. Perhaps we should include the makers of communion vessels, usually important-looking cups and plates of silver or with gold plating. They would find the sacraments of use. So might carvers or builders of what some churches call "baptismal fonts," stands that hold basins into which ordinary water is poured and from which, after the sacrament, water again gets poured, perhaps on the ground. Beyond that it is hard to figure out why sacraments should be important.

Within the faith community, however, they are very important. God can "save" the infant whose parents neglected to bring her to the font or church or river, though the command, encouragement, and promise are so strong that few responsible parents would want to be casual. The adult who presents herself as one who is coming to faith or coming in faith, ready for baptism, is not likely to call baptism "unimportant." Similarly, when a community of faith gathers to hear the Word of God, it also finds it important to see and say that the promise of grace is especially rich and vividly realized when people do not just sit there and hear a message but rather get to come forward, form a table or a circle, and in faith eat together. Millions have testified that such life in common, expressed at the font or the table, provides a most rich experience in the whole of spiritual life, even as they realize that it is different because of the special gifts and promises that come with it, thanks to the words of Jesus. So they find it important.

The sacraments are important also precisely because their elements are visible and tangible. One might think of them as being comparable to other aids to the imagination: visual aids, PowerPoint presentations, encounters with substances through touch and taste. Yet they are more than reminders or aids or something to be observed in order to promote something else. They call for obedience. With the Word of God, they offer benefits of grace and anticipate eternal life: one who is baptized becomes a child of God forever; one eats the banquet that Jesus was so eager to eat to receive gifts of life. Some have pondered what is different about the grace received in the sacraments over against the grace received in the Word. Answer: Grace is grace. However, we become aware of it and receive it in a different way in the sacraments.

Many a pastor who is "administering" the sacrament and many a baptized non-pastor, non–"office" holder, will comment on how at the Lord's Table as they hand out the bread or pour the wine they see eyes swell with tears—sometimes tears of joy, as they remember those who have gone ahead of them and are pictured at the heavenly banquet, and sometimes of sorrow over sins and struggles that the sacrament addresses. Baptism and the Lord's Supper are not "mere" signs of grace, symbols of the spiritual world in the material world. They *are* more than they *are not* something else. With the Word, they *are* grace givers. One German theologian used a strange grammatical construction in order to make something of this clear: when one receives the Word or participates in the sacraments, something happens—"it does not *not* happen." That happening is important, as it reaches to the core of Christian life and connects the human with a creating, redeeming, and holiness-making God.

Add to all this that sacraments are important as expressions of Christian community in a world of isolated, lonely, often seemingly abandoned and overlooked people. Baptism "works" when it is administered in a maternity ward to a child threatened with death, with no one present but a pastor or a baptizing nurse, or sometimes with only parents there to witness. Some Christians schedule baptism at off-hours, not in public worship, at times when "Grandma and Grandpa" can come. Most of the time, however, families who present a child or adults who are being baptized want to see the event as a form of public witness. The community, the congregation, sees and believes and cares. Similarly, believers often receive bread and wine alone, as in an emergency ward or on a deathbed or a battlefield. Ideally, however, "Communion" is not only the "communion of bread and wine with body and blood," but also the communion of believers among whom their Lord is present. These rites are too important to be hidden, rendered private, covered up—though the gift of grace can come with them in any setting or circumstance. Community at Communion, therefore, is important.

64. Why Do Lutherans Baptize Babies?

Why not? Lutherans are tempted to ask and often do ask. Why withhold from the littlest child the gifts of grace that come with baptism by water and in connection with the Word of God? Lutherans do not believe, indeed they *emphatically* don't believe, that what humans do makes the sacrament a sacrament. Baptism is not an achievement but a gift, and perhaps those who witness infant baptism can see best that no physical or spiritual achievement is being celebrated. What, we have to ask, can a two-hour- or two-week-old baby "bring" or wear as a merit badge or flaunt as a certificate of accomplishment?

It would be rude and crude, unthinking and unfeeling, however, to answer the question "Why do Lutherans baptize babies?" as abruptly as I did a paragraph ago with a word, "Why not?" Those who question the practice tend to be serious, often very serious people who take the sacrament seriously. Baptists and "Anabaptists"—the Reformation-era word for "re-baptizers" such as Mennonites and members of the Church of the Brethren— need to be heard. They reserve baptism until a child becomes old enough to think for herself, to make decisions by and for himself, to decide to stand before a congregation and the world, ready to serve as a witness to that world. An infant cannot do that. Further, connecting baptism with reasoned obedience is impossible in the case of the child "before the age of reason" when obedience is only that of parents and guardians, godparents and sponsors, who bring the child for baptism. Third, those who question baptism of infants want to make clear, to make a statement, that baptism is not a magic act, some wizardry that gets performed to induce miracles.

As a postscript, I might add the most fought-over feature through twenty centuries of Christian life: the New Testament in its accounts of Jesus' command and the disciples' follow-up does not specify that infants are to be baptized, just as it does not say they are not to be baptized. Very serious Christians from the church father Tertullian to one of the greatest twentieth-century theologians, Karl Barth, raised questions about the baptism of infants, and some who stood in traditions where their fellows did such baptizing stepped back from it and stopped doing it. Were they being literalists, or were the baptizers of infants being so?

To back this argument, one set of Christians made a point of the times the apostles noted the presence of faith in Jesus Christ and *then* baptized. The baptizers of infants noted the times in which whole households were baptized by apostles or those who followed them. Whole households almost certainly included infants, who should have been named as those to be excepted. It is not that baptizing a whole household included infants, if something physical like running in the Olympics or standing for Ph.D.

exams were in the offing. No, baptizing infants was the opposite of measuring the physicality of Olympic runners or the intellect of those who stand for examinations. Precisely because baptism offers gifts and effects promises, such baptizing Christians delight in showing what it exemplifies and does.

At the same time, when the believing community hears the words commanding baptism and the promise that goes with it at the time when the water gets poured or splashed or the infant is dunked, that community—beginning with the parents and family and the intimate circles around them—must take seriously its role in realizing the promises. The child is to grow into the meanings that may be symbolized with the baptismal robe that is too large for a tiny baby, or with the beauty of a diamond too precious for the baby to realize its worth. "Growth in grace" is always a corollary of baptism. Parents and godparents make pledges, "vows," that are sacred. The gathering is made up of people who are part of God's covenant, and the child becomes part of that covenant at baptism.

Once upon a time almost all Lutherans spoke of confirmation as a later rite, not calling it a sacrament because it confers no new blessings, but it does allow for people seriously to revisit their baptismal promises and make them their own in another way. Whether the rite is called confirmation or not, growing, reasoning children do affirm their baptism and take on their obligations or realize the life of grace in new ways when they speak up for themselves. Restraint about associating confirmation with adolescence is encouraged in some Lutheran churches where, too often, the congregation has seen the young people and their families considering confirmation as a kind of "graduation rite" comparable to junior high school ceremonies, seeing it as a charter for being done with Christian teaching and observance. If such a rite suggests that affirming baptism is other than to be a daily act or something stressed on each Lord's Day, one should treat it with caution. Otherwise, celebrate.

Too quickly I passed over the word "daily" in the lines above. Here is a point Lutherans are learning to stress after many of them had long been neglectful. Martin Luther made a recommendation that believers should begin their day by reference to baptism. To quote from an appendix to his Small Catechism: "In the morning, as soon as you get out of bed, you are to make the sign of the holy cross and say: 'God the Father, Son, and Holy Spirit watch over me. Amen.'" Then follows a little recommended ceremony including the Apostles' Creed and the Lord's Prayer, and perhaps a little additional prayer. Finally—get this!—"you are to go to your work joyfully." Note two things: First, the sign of the cross is not a sacrament but only a sign, a gesture that helps one bring back the story of what Jesus has done on the cross and through baptism. Make that sign or not, one might say, but do *something* to make the life of baptism vivid!

Second, this signing of the cross relates to a theme Luther developed in that catechism on the basis of Paul's writing in Romans 6:3–4: "[Baptism] means that our sinful self, with all its evil deeds and desires, should be drowned through *daily* repentance; and that day after day a new self should arise to live with God in righteousness and purity forever" (emphasis added).

A postscript is in order here: some of the sixteenth-century Lutheran Confessions speak of "confession" as a third sacrament. For a variety of reasons, some confessors in our time also like to think of confession as a sacrament: because the Lutheran Confessions sometimes did, to elevate the use of confessing of sins, and to show that defining a sacrament is not a precise act. (With confession, one of the features, a visible sign such as water or bread and wine, is missing.) Rather than make a fuss about the term, Lutherans do stress the act of confessing sins and the pronouncing of absolution, announcing that God has "absolved" and washed away the sin that blocked free access of God and grace to the individual heart.

65. I Do Not Remember My Baptism as an Infant. Can I be Rebaptized?

No, emphatically not, is the Lutheran answer. Lutherans say this not to thwart the desire of earnest and spiritually hungry adults who want to stress the meaning and value of baptism, but to make clear that the meaning and value of baptism do not depend on "remembering" the event in the way one remembers learning to ride a bicycle or mastering how to read or enjoying Mother's cooking. One "remembers" baptism not once in a repeated and renewed rite, but daily and in every act of repentance. If Lutherans started a new custom and became "Anabaptists," re-baptizers, they would be undercutting the understanding of baptism itself, in their contexts, and implicitly suggesting that all who were "only" baptized as infants were not "really" and "fully" baptized. In baptism, to use a term from John 3:3, they were "born from above"—a word translated "born again" in some texts and minds—and one cannot have that happen more than once, just as physical birth can happen only once. All this gets reported in the Gospel story in which an inquiring Jew asks Jesus how he could be born "from above" or "born again."

Believing all this and saying so is again to affirm what Lutherans and Catholics and all infant-baptizing Christians believe; it is not designed as an in-your-face assault on Baptists. If a child who was baptized grows up and joins a Baptist church, he or she will be "immersed"—the Baptist form of baptism—but that is not rebaptism. Baptists consider that the earlier event was not a baptism at all. *Now*, in their view, they are baptizing. A corollary of the Lutheran view that one is baptized only once is this: anyone baptized "in the name of the Father and of the Son and of the Holy Spirit"—the New Testament prescription—is baptized. Lutherans do not "re-baptize" Catholics or Presbyterians or others who become part of Lutheran congregations.

66. What Happens in the Lord's Supper?

First, we should pay a bit of attention to the name. If you look at the index in *The Book of Concord*, the fat book of sixteenth-century creedal statements of "Confessions" of the Lutherans, you will see scores upon scores of references to the "Lord's Supper." If you look up "Holy Communion" or "Eucharist," the index will say, "See Lord's Supper." That term with its time-of-day reference, used even when the sacrament is observed early in the morning at breakfast time, tends to be the preference of Lutherans, though none have anything against "Holy Communion," and nervousness about "Eucharist" is dissipating. Let's take a moment to discuss these.

There are good reasons to stress the term "Communion," because it alludes to the "communion" of earthly elements and the divine body and blood of Jesus, just as it accents the coming together and enjoyment of the common life among "communicants," which is what Lutherans call those who present themselves at the Lord's Table. Fine. The word "Eucharist" was not much used by Protestants for centuries, but it has come to be favored in the ecumenical era, where it picks up a stress as old as the first supper, where Jesus "gave thanks, and broke bread." The Greek word behind "Eucharist" appears fifty-five times in the New Testament. Early Christians often used the term. Those who favor it now stress that at the heart of Christian response to God's grace is the example and word of Jesus himself, who as he broke bread "gave thanks." The concept of divine generosity is so rich and the reasons to respond to it so vivid at the Lord's Table, that his word helps protect something valuable among Lutherans: to stress that "we" the people bring nothing to the table but hungry hearts, and God gives all, for which the people give thanks.

For historic reasons "the Lord's Supper" tends to be the favored designation among many kinds of Christians. Lutherans have a special reason for stressing it. Luther wrote that while the meaning of the Lord's Supper is the same in any circumstance, the context helps foster the imagination of those who celebrate it. He said that when seeking guidance about its celebration, we can imagine whether in a cave or a chapel or a cathedral, Christians should seek to measure what they are doing by what the Gospels say went on in the upper room the night before Jesus died. Such counsel was to assure a stress on the story of the supper in the context of Jesus' forthcoming death and his promise to those gathered that he would eat this meal in the coming kingdom. And this counsel also helps feature the fact that the words of blessing on the bread, the command to the disciples, and the promise of forgiveness would be highlighted. The term "the Lord's Supper" is one way of accenting all this.

The question is, "What happens in the Lord's Supper?" Once again, I turn to that strange linguistic turn from a theologian: "Something really happens; it does not *not* happen." The Lord's Supper is not just a story, a ceremony, a reminiscence, something that will give Christians something more to argue about. The Lord's Supper is a happening in which God reaches down, Christ is present, and the Holy Spirit is enacting that presence. So one can never attach adjectives or adverbs or other words like "mere," as in "the 'mere' representation of the body and blood of Christ" or "nothing but" bread and wine. Sometimes Lutherans speak of "the real presence of Christ" in the sacrament, though among them are those who say the term does not have much backing in history. What does "real" mean there? Why not just say "the presence"? In Christian belief, Lutheran style, the risen and ascended Lord, who, as the creed says, "sits at the right hand of the Father" and is "omnipresent," is present in the bread and wine and company of believers. (The word "company" is based on words that signal eating bread together!)

What happens? How can this be? Lutherans like to use the category of "mystery" here, not because they want to kick up dust in the air and then complain that they cannot see. Instead, "mystery" is a way of speaking that goes beyond talk of a "problem." Problems have solutions: here the problem is, how shall we speak of ordinary bread, really ordinary bread and wine, as being the body and blood of Christ? Some have tried to be helpful by borrowing words from philosophy and have talked at times of "transubstantiation" or "consubstantition." The imported concept of "substance" hidden in both of those words might solve a problem for philosophers, but it has little to do with the meaning of a meal in an upper room in Jerusalem two thousand years ago. Ask the disciples about "substance" and "trans-" and "con-" and they would do you the service of looking utterly puzzled.

Mysteries, unlike problems, do not have solutions. They have depth, they are fathomless, they invite people into the boundless. Lutherans sometimes try to picture what they witness to in the Lord's Supper. Many a child in catechism class has dealt with presuppositions such as "In, with, and under the bread and wine they receive the body and blood." So they might draw a loaf and a picture of Jesus broken on the cross and an arrow to suggest "in." Or they draw a cup and a picture of Jesus losing blood from his nail-pierced body and draw something that suggests that "with" bread and wine this body and blood are present. Or "under" the pictures of bread and wine they draw the body and blood, perhaps not knowing that they are inheriting language of revelation: "under" the bread and wine, hidden, as it were—Lutherans like the language of God's "hiddenness"—are the body and blood.

Nice try. Many of us find these helpful, but not capable of eliminating the mystery of the presence. At some point Lutherans tend to despair of explaining the unexplainable and just plain enjoy God's gift. They used to define themselves negatively: we are *not* magic-minded like Catholics as they deal with substance or minimalists like the Reformed and others who liked to say that the elements were merely symbolic or representative. They move on then to realize that in this meal the same Word that hung on the cross and is now risen, the same Word that appears in the words of the original Lord's Supper, is keeping the promise of being with the disciples and followers "as often as they eat this bread and drink this cup," thus "showing" the Lord's body.

Lutherans, like other Christians, approach the Lord's Table having examined themselves, having isolated and discerned and regretted their sins, having resolved to walk in the new life that baptism signals, and having shown readiness to receive grace through and with these visible signs. Since Luther and Lutherans believe that at the beginning and in the end, the gospel is about the forgiveness of sins, they stress Jesus' remembered word that all this is "for the forgiveness of sins." And since they are at Communion, they also experience new awareness of the "church" made up of those who have gone before or who are far away and those who will succeed them. The Lord's Supper is in its own way a futuristic activity, since those who celebrate it are proclaiming "the Lord's death until he comes" (1 Corinthians 11:26). They look forward to the heavenly banquet, one of Jesus' terms for the future beyond mortality and with God. And they get much impetus for the ethics from the Lord's Supper, as they are to extend the circle of communion and live renewed Christ-serving lives.

67. Do We Really Eat and Drink the "Body and Blood" of Jesus in the Lord's Supper?

Yes, depending upon the definition of the word "really." "Really" does not mean ingesting the corpuscles and cells of Jesus of Nazareth. However, Lutherans get nervous when words like "nothing but" or "mere" or "merely" get attached to the bread and wine. Such terms don't cover the subject. What is "mere"? Is anything mere? One literary scholar said it was a fateful moment when in an argument with Luther in 1529 the Swiss reformer Huldreich Zwingli attached the concept of "mere" to the bread and wine. He was being a modern. That is, he was disassociating a symbol from what it symbolized. Luther appeared to Zwingli and others who sided with him to be a medieval man, recalling a time when the symbol and the reality were easily matched. Ever since, said that critic, moderns have been trying to find a way back, to make the symbol *not* an arbitrary representation—as if Jesus could just as well have said "pizza" and "Coke" instead of "bread" and "wine," but an organically connected reality of bread and body, wine and blood.

So Lutherans can answer that, yes, they believe we "really" do this eating, but they don't believe that philosophical answers to the question of "really" are satisfying, and they do believe that the word "mere" has to be dropped. That sentence sounds rather negative and argumentative: Lutherans like to *celebrate* the Lord's Supper, and sooner or later, preferably sooner, they stop defining and enjoy enjoying, inviting others.

68. Can Unconfirmed Children and Non-Church Members Take Communion?

That question made more sense at a time when Lutherans turned confirmation, especially at the time of adolescence, into a sharply defining act. With that ceremony you were "in" or "out." Some still do observe confirmation that way, and then can answer quite simply that "unconfirmed children *cannot* take Communion." Other Lutherans, trying to get away from the concept of confirmation as a figurative earning of a diploma or an adolescent rite of passage, tend to "relativize" this by asking instead what one is out to protect or to defend when discussing who is to approach the Lord's Table. In the early church, when people risked their lives as they became Christians, the fences around the table were high. Part of a worship service was a "mass for catechumens," those "on the way," who then found the door slammed as the "mass for the faithful" went on among those who, it was thought, were ready for the divine mysteries and to prepare themselves to spread the message or give their lives.

In colonial New England the Puritans spoke of "fencing the table," building a figurative wall around it, and denying entrance to all who could not produce a token or a ticket. Lutherans often have spoken of their favoring or insisting on "closed Communion," which suggests that "fencing" or, now more frequently, "close Communion," which pictures the ready and faithful to be huddled close to each other around the table of their Lord. The intention behind such fencing and closing and being close is not something to be argued here, or mentioned in order to show disdain for fellow Lutherans or other Christians. It is clear that they intended and intend something positive in something that looks so negative, to work toward "including" after a process of "excluding." They quote one word from the Bible that says no one should eat or drink without "discerning" the Lord's body, because if they do, they risk damnation. Whatever else that meant or means, it cannot have meant something intellectual, like passing a final examination in a confirmation or adult class. It cannot mean expecting those who approach the Lord's Table to give an account of Luther versus Zwingli, or trans- versus consubstantiation. If it did, Lutherans would stop giving communion to the nearly comatose or to people with profound mental disabilities. (Chaplains suggest that few communicants give evidence of "discerning" and "understanding" more aptly than do some with Down syndrome or severe retardation at homes for those with mental disabilities!) Fencing or closing or excluding might have occurred to teach hunger for confirmation and sacramental life. It may have been designed to stress the seriousness of the act of communing, and may not always have meant what the excluded so often witness: not "care of souls," but "we're better than you," a very un–Holy Communion idea.

Leaving all that argument and name-calling behind, we move to the positive: what do most Lutherans expect of anyone who approaches the table? Some of them offer the bread to infants on the assumption that they are part of the communing congregation and will grow into the meanings even as they grow into their baptism. Others wait until a child is five or six and have a special instruction, so children are not casual and utterly uncomprehending as they partake of the Lord's Supper. Most still associate communing with some version of confirmation, stressing here some historical, theological, communal, and moral meanings of the sacramental life.

What about "non-church members"? This could mean "non-Lutheran church members." A large minority of Lutherans in

North America restrict attendance, as they did in a nineteenth-century "Rule": "Lutheran altars and pulpits for Lutherans only." Most, however, have moved into the ecumenical age and believe they are reverting to early Christian practices by saying that all baptized Christians who are living in the discipline and responsible life of another Christian congregation are welcome at the table. They remind all that it is "the Lord's Table" and not "the Lutheran table." One cannot write a book of this sort without recognizing that Lutheran practices differ on some issues, and especially on this one. Inquirers about joining Lutheran churches should and will inquire about this. Visitors will remain confused. Long-term members will have taken the questions about "welcome" into consideration as they become or remain part of particular congregations or jurisdictions.

chapter eleven

Christian Life

69. What Do Lutherans Believe about Saints?

It's time to bring up saints, since they play such a part in Christian life and thought. So many churches, including Lutheran ones, are named after saints, such as "St. Luke" or "St. Paul" or, more rarely, but in place, "St. Mary." These are usually figures from the Bible. On occasion one can find a "St. Martin's"—not Martin Luther, but the saint of the day of little Martin's baptism—or St. Lawrence. All Lutherans celebrate All Saints Day, and many sing, "For all the saints, who from their labors rest. . . ." In such cases they are talking about people who have died and, in resurrected life, are in the presence of God, thanks to the grace of God. Preachers will often refer to ordinary members of the congregation as saints, knowing full well that few are listed in the ranks of the extraordinary doers of good. It is clear from all these usages that for Lutherans, saintliness is a mark of many a Christian life, but sainthood as such is derived from God's mercy, not a mark of human achievement.

So what about the extraordinary people honored as saints in the church year? Lutherans do not shy away from thanking God for St. Francis, the humble servant, or pious St. Benedict or St. Bernard of Clairvaux, who is identified as the author of several favorite hymns. In all such cases our remembering them is a way of honoring people through whom God has worked in extraordinary ways. They are set up as models, errant human beings whose virtues live on and are to inspire believers today.

Two things Lutherans will not do. First, they will not see the saints as high achievers who have earned the honors shown them or the special favor of God, who operates democratically, one might say, by treating all persons equally as sinners and as saved. Second, they will not claim access to the saints who are dead and may be in glory, which means that they also will not use them to intercede before God. The Reformers of the sixteenth century swept the shelf bare of such figures who, as exemplary as they were, could not "put in a word" for people in need now. Lutherans know that there are saints for midwives and workmen, people in desperate circumstances (as who is not often?), and so many more. The Scriptures make clear that between God and humans there is *one* mediator, Jesus Christ. To think of others is to distract from the complete act of love worked by Jesus Christ on the cross. To think of others is to suggest that the believer cannot have direct access to God as Jesus promised them they could when he spoke his words about prayer in the Bible without mentioning the prayers of saints.

In sum, Lutherans believe that they should be as democratic about sainthood as God is, using the term, properly defined, as applying to their fellow members. Lutherans suggest that people might show more regard for each other, more readiness to include others in prayer, if they would look down the pew or the register of members and know that baptized so-and-so is really St. Adam Schroeder, St. Eve Morrison, St. Mary Murphy—in whom God is working good things toward good ends.

70. Do Lutherans Believe That Christians Can Attain Perfection in This Life?

Simple questions demand simple answers. For this one, the answer is no. This is the case because "perfection" in such contexts means something that results from trying, striving, achieving, facing up to the evils in one and eliminating whatever holds her back from being perfect as Jesus Christ was and is—the only human who did not "attain" perfection but came among humans as the perfect messenger and Son of God. Having said that, Lutherans also note that seeking to be *nearer* perfection is in place; they speak of it as "growth in grace," so that the inspirer and enabler of steps along the way is always God, never the grasping and eager human.

Some Christian traditions, the Wesleyan (as in Methodist) among them, do speak of perfection as both a goal and somehow an attainable reality, but they surround this speaking with so many qualifiers that it remains true: Wesleyans sin, too. Rather than try to get inside what they mean when they speak of it, Lutherans find it better to picture, not how other humans look on them, but how God does. Here Lutherans have a special twist, but they alone are not the ones who have it. The famous Reformed theologian Karl Barth wrote a shelf-long book series titled *Church Dogmatics*. He was a formidably learned man, whose footnotes could go on for pages. One of these or one cluster of these was translated into a book called *Christ and Adam*. Barth argued or noticed that, of course, we all see each other "in Adam," as participants in human finitude and sin. Christian congregations put locks on their doors, bond their church treasurer, and have more than one person count offerings. They assume that their children are not innocent. They are children of Adam.

Barth went on to say that Christians would do as well if they thought of each other as being "in Christ." Now let's switch quickly to Luther, who anticipated that point of view when he spoke so regularly of the human as *simul iustus et peccator* (at the same time "made just" and also still a sinner). Lutherans stress this duality so much that it has become a kind of distinctive mark in ecumenical Christianity. A few years ago, the representatives of the Lutheran World Federation signed a kind of "bury the hatchet" document with official Roman Catholicism on the disputed teaching of "justification by faith." This was a giant step forward in ecumenical relations. However, not only critics of the signing, who want every "i" dotted and "t" crossed, but many other Lutherans did insist that the task of coming to entente was still unfinished. This was because Catholic teaching about what remains of the image of God in sinful humans gives God something to work with. No, say Lutherans, finding their resource in the Bible, human sin meant the smashing of the image of God. Justification by grace through faith means not a rebuilding of an image by God, but a new creation. They therefore believe that when God looks upon the Christians "in Adam," nothing is satisfying, and not even the first step to perfection has occurred. When God looks upon the baptized believer "in Christ," we can speak of that person as from that perspective "perfect" as Christ was, and Luther could even say that such a Christian is to be not *as* Christ but *a* Christ to the neighbor.

The downside of this interpretation of the Bible is that it deprives believers of bragging rights or claims of perfection. The upside is that they get the liberating, ennobling, and empowering sense that God can work with them as privileged children in the kingdom.

71. If We Are Christians, Do We Have to Obey God's Law?

Yes, indeed, always yes. Christians cannot conceive of God as being half-serious in giving commands. In the Sermon on the Mount, Jesus is quoted as giving the command to "be perfect" (Matthew 5:48). He did not say, "I would like to whisper a hint in the form of a suggestion that might be a seconding of a motion that you try to be a bit better than you were before you heard this command." The Ten Commandments make commands, of course. Jesus renders them even more urgent and severe when he says, "You have heard that it was said . . . but I say unto you." People who like to use the concept of absolutes, absent though it is from the Bible, have to say that the commands are absolutes. God is not a relativist teaching relativism, a "just keep trying" and "never mind" and "all is well" pronouncing sort.

Lutherans are just as emphatic in saying that no human other than Jesus, not Mary or John the Baptist or Paul, kept the commandments. Instead, Jesus stands in their place and by his perfect obedience has won a new situation before God for believers. So the New Testament can speak at times about the law having been done away with, and thus Christians are to live by grace and in freedom from the tyranny of the law. Christians set out to keep the law because it is God's law, because Jesus fulfilled the law with love rather than smashing it. Properly seen, the law can be used in the larger society just as the biblical stories suggest it was designed to serve among the nomadic children of Israel. The law commands all not to steal, to lie, to kill, to covet, and the world is better off when such a command is repeated and its source believed in.

Lutheran teaching accents a theme from the Bible that is often understressed elsewhere. It sees the law of God as a tyrant in the context of humans being made just. In a classic formula, *lex semper accusat* (the law always accuses). It shows how great is the gap between what a holy God expects and what an unholy human at her best can deliver. It drives believers from the notion that they can please God by having kept the law. It drives people who are thus accused to run for mercy to Christ, who did keep the law.

So don't expect Lutherans to relativize the law of God or to subvert it. They simply want to block notions that keeping the law is the way to please God and to win God's favor and salvation.

72. Does God Answer Prayer?

Yes, God answers prayer, because God says God does, and that ought to settle it. Jesus emphatically urges and commands disciples to pray, and other biblical writers regularly urged prayer, and prayed. Why urge something futile, and why command something that leaves hearers frustrated and feeling foolish? Having said that, no humane writer, including one in the evangelical Lutheran tradition, could be cavalier about answering such a question and making it seem as if, in a magic act, God commands prayer, so Christians pray, and hence everything will turn out as the praying ones demand or expect. (By the way, "demanding" is not out of bounds, since Jesus asks his disciples to insist on seeing the promises of God realized.) Anyone who has eyes to see can see that not all prayers are fulfilled as the prayerful one wishes. I might pray for a Rolls-Royce and not even get a used car. I might pray for recovery from illness and still die. I might pray to overcome temptation and it keeps coming back—as Luther experienced and so clearly taught it would.

Jesus not only commanded prayer but lived the life of prayer and set an example. And the contexts of his prayer teaches much about what hearers of the teaching might do and might expect. He prayed that the cup of suffering be taken from him in Gethsemane the night before he was killed, yet he was killed. He prayed that that cup be taken away and said, "Not what I want, but what you want" (Mark 14:36), but he *kept on praying.* Prayer for him was constant communication with God, and answering prayer was an ongoing activity of the human's conversation partner in prayer. The agonized conversation turned from prayer to questioning when on the cross he asked why God had forsaken him. Then, according to the Gospels, he commended himself to his Father, who, in Christian teaching, vindicated Jesus by raising him from the dead. Telling the story as I have just done is one way of showing that Christian teaching on prayer is difficult. It would be easy if the Scriptures taught us to think of prayer as one-half of a magic act. It would be easier if prayer were always obviously answered in the form and at the time we want. Yet it does not work out that way.

Rather than apologize for God in the cases where prayers have apparently not been answered, it is well to focus on the experience of millions, perhaps billions, of Christians who did recognize answered prayer and changed their lives in the context of the gratitude this inspires. People who are not subject to illusion or delusion, hardheaded scientific skeptical sorts who have turned their lives over to God in prayer, acknowledge answered prayer. They represent one kind of problem: how to make sense of their certitude that God has heard their prayers. The same people on other occasions or other people in similar occasions, however, represent another kind of problem: that of apparently unanswered prayer.

Most of them are not comforted by the notion sometimes advanced by well-meaning friends that they have prayed wrongly for the wrong thing, or too briefly for boons that take a long time. They are not content to be told that they are playing a lottery and that a capricious God, like an Oriental potentate, rolls the dice and chooses to do something for someone and hold back from another. Often they are not pleased to be told that they are being schooled in patience, while others make a quick killing and get what they want. It really hurts to be told that they do not deserve to be helped because they are not good enough—and if they are being told that, it goes against the gospel.

What seems best is for them to concentrate on aspects of divine revelation that do not overstress philosophy. Philosophy likes the "omni-" words, as in God being omniscient, omnipresent, omnipotent, and more. Not that God is not all-knowing, all-present, all-powerful. It simply is a teaching or a conclusion that does not match experience, including that of many in the Bible. The God revealed to Christians has created a universe for them and planted them in it. They are creatures of nature, subject to natural disasters and universal experiences, like dying. They are creatures with a will, which they can pray to have directed to serve the purposes of God, even as they can make mistakes and bring on some misfortunes.

In the end, no explanations satisfy. Better is the counsel of Jesus to continue praying, thus keeping the divine-human conversation going, during which one experiences many versions of God's activity, knowing that on earth no one will get satisfying answers to all questions.

73. Does God Heal Today?

Certainly great numbers of believers believe that God heals today, and saying that is the beginning of an answer to the question. It is quite natural for Lutherans to join other Christians in believing that it is worthwhile to pray to God for healing, because in response God heals, in a variety of forms. One can postpone the hard answers to a hard question by elaborating on all the meanings of "healing," but then finding along the way that some of these answers are not distractions but are helpful insights into the ways of God toward humans.

Thus God heals in the case of the current disease, the pain of separation from God. It is not diverting or cute to say that. Christians recall a biblical story where friends presented a paralyzed person for healing, and Jesus forgave his sins. Criticized or questioned, he asked why onlookers were mystified. Healing physical illness was not difficult, and Jesus would soon heal. For a perfect God to forgive sins is more expensive and trying for God. God would work that miracle and forgive, and thus heal. Is it not diverting to say that God heals through medicine and care facilities? These are gifts of the Creator and of people in research and delivery of care who may not even realize that they are performing God's healing. A third way is to translate "healing" to mean "reconciling," repairing broken human institutions and relations. That is true, but not fully satisfying, because the godless can often heal in this pattern.

At the opposite extreme are the many Christians, Pentecostal or not, on television or not, who believe in a special way about a special sort of miracles. Bring a paralyzed person or one whose body is filled with malignant tumors. Have an evangelist-healer do something and—*voila!*—there is healing. That is satisfying to the televised congregation but raises skepticism about trickery among critics. Such "miraculous" healing can go on in hospitals and other institutions of mercy or where there is home care. Rather than dismiss sudden turns out of hand, Christians are often more ready to be modest and grateful, inspired by what they find to be remarkable.

In the face of all the half-answers and frustrations of those who seek philosophically and medically improved interpretations of healing, Christians of Lutheran-type outlooks stress the need for supporting institutions of research, medicine, and nursing care. Some Muslim teaching matches that of much Christian teaching: medicine *is* the instrument of divine healing. Meanwhile, Lutherans will not rule out miraculous healing, but they will understress it, in part because it gives anxiety to those not being healed—they ask what they have done wrong, or they judge those who are getting the favors—and in part because the biblical record, including in the face of Jesus, shows many un-healed who persevere in faith.

74. How Do We Know the Will of God?

Abraham Lincoln, no church member but a profoundly religious figure, during the Civil War counseled both sides, but especially his own Union side—the Confederacy would not have listened—not to claim that the will of God was on their side. They should instead seek to discern the mysterious will of the Almighty and seek to follow it. He used the right adjective when he spoke of that will as "mysterious." That meant not that it was "unknowable," but instead that the depth and bounds and riches of God were too unimaginably expansive for anyone to claim a "knowing" hold on it. Certainly the will of God is known—and not only generally. We are to "fear and love God," as Luther's Small

Catechism affirms with respect to each of the Ten Commandments. Even more specifically we can know the will of God, since it is connected to all of the commandments and to the petitions (one-phrase prayers) in the Lord's Prayer and is revealed throughout Scripture.

What gets more difficult is discerning the will of God in specific cases. Is it God's will that this country should go to war, or join the global society, or engage in stem-cell research? Even to pose such controversial items shows how hard it is to back one's claim that he has discerned the mysterious will of God. People on both sides of most issues in politics, economics, and culture try to know the will of God and claim to act on it. They are often careful and prayerful, sincere and humble, but still confident that they "know." So do equally sincere and conscientious Christians on the other side of issues concerning war, economics, and medical research. What this amounts to is not the need to end searches for the will of God, but the need to be humble, aware of other viewpoints, and ready to post a sign: "Handle with Care."

The first step in the attempt to know God's might will sound like a cliché, a bit of advice routinely handed out, namely, pray. A life of prayer brings one into increasing congruence with a God who speaks and offers counsel out of God's will for others, including the one who prays. Often those who have prayed intensely speak of coming to a stage of discernment and summoning of will.

Next, Lutherans join others in trying to know about the psychology of decision-making, so they will say that it is important to gain perspective, to summon what can be known and to move from there. Third, "try it on." Lutherans are to be an adventurous, risk-taking people, not intimidated and timid as many of the caricatures of their ways suggest. Venture, they will be told, and be ready with Plan B if Plan A does not appear to be satisfying. Offer yourself humbly and in a spirit of readiness to live with disappointment, surprise, or unmerited good. Finally, don't claim too much: tuck away in your own mind and memory what you have discerned as the will of God. Overadvertisement calls attention to the advertiser, not to the hidden God who is revealed in diverse ways.

75. What Is My Christian "Vocation"?

You will get clues to answers for this question by asking it often, listening well, trying answers on for size, and being ready to revise. It is not hard to answer, "What is my work?" or "What is my job?" or "What is my career?" Whatever one comes up with is easily revisable: change careers or even professions on the basis of whim, good or bad breaks, whom you know, and the choice of climate. Vocation is deeper, harder to reach. Lutherans really love the concept and the question. Sure of his vocation, his calling, his way of life with his name figuratively stamped on it, Martin Luther first thought his vocation was to be a monk. When he left the monastery, however, he had lost his work, job, and career. He could carry much of his profession out the monastery door with him. He made use of the skills, knowledge, and habits of an Old Testament professor of exegesis and interpretation. He discovered along the way, however, that his calling to serve God as a monk no longer served God.

Soon he was preaching in evangelical contexts, helping define the reform of the church, marrying and loving Katie and the family, in a new vocation: being a minister of the gospel and a reformer of the church. There were no job descriptions to go with the last of these, the one for which he is most well known and the one that lasted. Professions come and go, but vocations last. One finds his or her vocation by trial and error and by learning through many challenges and discoveries, more than by hearing voices and interpreting *them* as the call of God. This vocation, which in Luther's case had probably been hidden all the years that he was trying to find himself as Martin Luther, now exposed him to the world. Vocation, calling, belongs not only to the monastery but to the world.

Those who give Lutherans a chance will hear a great deal about "vocation," since the followers of Luther in the tradition of Paul the apostle never think that all should have the same vocation, or that the vocation of the monk is "higher" than that of the diaper-changer. They will hear that they can get plenty of help from their pastor, from counselors, potential employers, family members, authors. They will make a point of it that the vocation is renewed daily when in the morning one repents of bad things and false starts, remembers baptism, and greets the future with resolve, not guilt, not worry. They will read biographies of others who kept finding dimensions of their calling, and consult books on how this concept of vocation might relate to that of other people. They will then follow up with *some* sense of a God-willed vocation but will be smart enough to learn how and when to take further steps.

chapter twelve

The Reign of God

76. Why Is Our View of the Future Important?

Humans cannot be unmindful of the future. As one philosopher put it, "We are beings-toward-death." That is, our humanity is measured not only from our conception or emergence from the womb, through daily activities, but always in the light of the fact that our present bodily existence will end. Consciously or unconsciously, we make decisions with the future in mind. Many invest in stocks or hope for Social Security and pension plans to kick in when we need them. Parents look at children and grandchildren and try to envision their future, the world into which they grow, and often try to help them plan for it. Married couples pledge "till death us do part," signaling even on a festal marriage day that the future of human life is not all open, that parting will come.

Humans in groups also think of various futures. They fight wars and seek peace so that their nation can live on. They build buildings to provide roofs over the heads of those in associations and clubs of which they are a part. Those who care greatly about institutions such as colleges and universities invest in them and hope for them. We try to provide for family members who will outlive us. Still, all that worrying, planning, and hoping, though it reveals much about human nature, pales to relative insignificance compared to thought about our personal futures.

The biblical portrayals of God show God to be the Creator of beginnings and the one who controls the ends of our earthly lives and receives us eternally. That is, time belongs to God, who alone knows the future. In some passages God is revealed as the power of the future, the Holy Spirit calls believers into futures, and Jesus is also depicted as one who assures followers that they are not to have care for the next day, just before he reveals that God is in command of the ages, beginnings, middles, and ends.

Thinking about the future usually prompts people to plan, to make provision, and sometimes to develop the illusion that they have the power over the future. A lecturer can speak on such subjects, for instance at an estate-planning seminar, and fall dead the next day, not being able to put to work anything he or she has imparted to others in the normal course of things, with an ordinary future in view.

Jesus Christ offers a different view of the future than the ones called "natural." We are not to worry about this life. God has turned to humans and given them a future and a hope. Most decisive among views of the future is the announcement that God, because of the work of Jesus Christ, has conquered death and removed reasons for believers to fear the future, something most of them in many ways are going to continue to do anyhow. They tend to seek and to find for themselves various more or less satisfactory and pleasing views of the future, despite the promise that positive futures await us.

77. What Do We Believe about the End of the World?

Here it is not a cheap evasion to say, "Wait and see!" No believer knows the end, has come back from it to report, or can do anything about the end. Christians believe the world will have a natural end, no matter what humans do to bring it on. Most consider that end to be so remote that they cannot be consumed with thinking about it. An evolutionist-minded futurist gave a lecture envisioning the future as the globe got colder or warmer, "two billion years from now." A member of the audience asked, "Did you say two *million* or two *billion* years?" He retold his view: two billion years. The audience member sighed: "Oh, good. For a moment I thought you had said two *million* years." Somehow our instinctive planning for the future or enjoyment of the present is conditioned by views of various lengths of time until the future.

It is also not a cheap answer to say that we don't know much about the end of the world. Christians can say that with the best of warrants, since in the Gospels Jesus is also mute about the end, saying that his Father had not given him the key to unlocking the future (Mark 13:32). Only the one he called "Abba" (Father) knew. Jesus would on occasion tell parables, vivid stories about divine judgment that awaited all. Sometimes he made it sound almost like a desperate game: God would come stealthily and suddenly, like a thief in the night. He told this to motivate people to settle affairs, be on their toes, repent, and be eager to the final day.

The scriptures in both Testaments use so many different ways to sound the alert about the future that it would be difficult to sort them out and pin them down until one came out with a single vision—something that all too many Christians are all too ready to do. What that variety of images serves to do is to stimulate imaginations and quicken moral energies for no matter what comes. Yet again in this brief chapter it is in place to say that we should be humble, that we are dealing with the impossible to imagine, that we should invoke the language of mystery. Were the future a problem to be solved, one could take a biblical puzzle and set out to solve it—again, as many try to do. The mystery of the end, however, is not a problem but something that has to be unveiled when the time comes, while those who look ahead cannot master it.

What do we know, if we believe the biblical pictures? We are told that there will *be* an end; things will not just follow event upon event in timeless and tireless fashion. No, things proceed and then: the end. Second, we are privileged to hear about this mystery that, whatever is to happen, God is in control. Humans may blow up God's creation through their folly and evil creations, or they may heat up the globe so much that everything on it will die. Still, even if the end is to come that sinful way, it will not occur beyond the scope of the Creator. Add to that the announcement that this end involves Jesus Christ. In Holy Communion services congregations shout:

Christ has died!
Christ is risen!
Christ will come again!

Some who say these words may, in the corner of their minds, have a picture from the Gospels or the writings of Paul that uses the kind of language and imagery humans can handle: of the heavens opening, of Jesus coming on clouds of glory to greet or be greeted by the saints. Such a version was easier to imagine when hearers and readers believed in a flat earth at the center of the universe. Now with the world being no more than a speckle of dust in a remote zone of ever-swirling spheres, other visions might serve better. Now people may turn to Old Testament pictures of the Day of the Lord. In all these pictures there is a sense that Jesus comes in glory in his resurrected presence, holding humans accountable in some sort of judgment—but recognizing and aiding his "saints," the sinners who have believed in him. Then the world may be consumed, or restored, or replaced—the pictures vary so much that one cannot line them up logically. It is also well to notice that most of these revelations come in the form of dreams, which always move dreamers far beyond the literal and the practical. And beyond the dreams, God the Lord of history will bring forth "a new heaven and a new earth." To ask whether that is literal or figurative is to try to peer beyond what is unfolded in the Bible.

78. When Will Jesus Come Again?

In the providence of God this coming again is hidden. So eager are humans to envision particular futures that they consult soothsayers or fortune-tellers and muse over messages of street-corner prophets who wear signboards announcing the imminence of the end. "Repent!" Probably every day since the biblical records were written and spread, someone or large groups of someones became specific and won followings as they spelled out in detail the "when." What all these millions of guessers and prophesiers have in common is this: *they have all been wrong.* The same can be said about those who are making the same pronouncement today: they are all wrong, they will all be wrong, they are playing God, and Jesus himself, in biblical accounts, does not want humans idly to play God.

It is not wrong to speak of an imminent end. Jesus did. The apostles did. The Gospels are full of accounts that suggest that those who lived with Jesus and heard his promises thought the end would come in their lifetimes. Yet most of them kept on living. We have heard of a modern end-times evangelist who wowed crowds with calls to repent, because it was likely that the world would end in a year or a day or a minute. "Buy my book, and learn more," was the pitch that followed. And then he might go on: "And so that this message can be preached for generations to come, write our Bible college into your will." Another, who prophesied that the world had to end within the generation after the birth of Israel, indeed, forty years thereafter, saw the fortieth year go by with nothing happening. He too sold millions of books with this message about the almost-instant end. We learned later that he plowed his proceeds into real estate, a kind of long-term investment. I mention this not to be snide but to try to keep a humane Christian view in mind: talk of the end can be a consolation and not a threat, something with which to stun audiences. Good news, again: the end is to be followed with the creation of God's new heaven and new earth. If we do not know exactly what that means, and admit it, good: the biblical version of the end is being grasped. We are catching on. We can teach our grandchildren so they can teach their grandchildren.

79. Do Lutherans Have to Worry about Being "Left Behind"?

Less than two centuries ago they would not have had such a worry because they had never heard the language about being "left behind." Most Christians still have not, though thanks to mass production of books and magazines and mass evangelists and mass media featuring televising of images, in some parts of the world the language about being "left behind" has become current—enough so that many ask their spiritual counselors and pastors about it. All-time bestsellers and highest-grossing films have featured the left-behind concept. It is hard to measure what all goes into the appeal. Some think that much of it appeals to certain Christians the same way science fiction and horror films appeal to the public. On-screen one can see Jesus speaking, and his words are like a sword that cuts people up, spilling their intestines, as their exposed agonies thrill the righteous.

Such imagery is the modern version of what medieval artists liked to portray: God judging, with half the people being cast into the devil's jaws and eternal flames and the others being planted in paradise. Somehow "we" always land on the benign side, assuming in the Middle Ages we were faithful at mass and made pilgrimages or in our time supported this or that evangelist. The people who have invented the "left behind" concept have a little bit of scripture to support them. In 1 Thessalonians 4:13–18 for a moment a window opens on scenes of people being "left behind" because they had not readied themselves for Jesus' coming to summon his saints into heaven. The "left behind" people do perform some services: Again, they remind us that there will be an end. They stress the importance of moral self-examination and spiritual readiness. They are not apathetic or adrift, as many non-believers or other-believers are. Because they are children of the gospel and believers in the good news in Christ, the fundamental view of all Christians ought to be to accept and enjoy what God has promised: that nothing shall separate us from the love of God in Christ Jesus.

80. What Do Lutherans Believe about the Millennium?

Were it not for the fact that on the second-to-last page of the long book called the Bible there is reference to a rule on earth by Jesus for a thousand years (Revelation 20:1–10), Lutherans would not think about it at all. The word appears in a writing that from page one identifies itself as a vision or a dream, and never pretends to be "literal" about the past or present or future. It delivers extremely provocative images, often of great poetic beauty. No doubt it was designed almost like a code language to give early Christians hope, probably because their life of faith in the Roman Empire was dangerous. Through the ages some small sects of Christians picked up on that language and made much of it. A few of these were around in Luther's day. He definitely believed that the world would end soon, so much so that he did not even think it was important to send missionaries into all the world. People should be faithful where the gospel was present. When Luther and the Lutherans heard of prophets of the end who got specific, as in speaking of a thousand-year rule, they ignored it, pooh-poohed it, or tried to refute those who proclaimed it.

Bible students in the British Isles picked up this language in the 1840s, as some of their Bible-student ancestors had done, and spread the word of their discovery so widely that, as many believed it, they helped enter new words and phrases into the vocabulary. Some were "premillennialists," believing that dire things about which Jesus spoke still had to come, and after that he would return for the thousand-year reign of peace. They currently predominate among the thousand-year calendar keepers. In the past couple of centuries those who were more optimistic, progressive, and programmatic were "postmillennialists." That is, they believed that if they worked hard, spread the Word, made converts, brought justice and mercy, and made the world attractive, Jesus would come for the thousand-year rule. They tended to be less "literalistic" in their claims, and many in their camps were or were seen as liberals.

Most Lutherans look on and listen in but would be classed as amillennialists: Jesus will come, Jesus will rule, but "a day in his sight is *like* a thousand years," and a thousand years are like a day. They are ready for whatever a judging and loving God has in store. It has been said that most premillennialists "give up on the world before God does," but Lutherans would want to be among those who accept the gifts of days and centuries and millennia as times of opportunity for service and praise.

81. What Is the "Resurrection of the Body"?

Christians in their creed affirm that Jesus is risen from the dead, and in the Apostles' Creed, after they have affirmed "the forgiveness of sins," they say that they believe in "the resurrection of the body, and the life everlasting." It has been said that whoever says the first line of the creed, "I believe in God, the Father almighty, creator of heaven and earth," is poised and ready to affirm the last: that the original Maker of the first creation fulfills promises and makes a new creation, one that involves the believing person. And involvement is of the whole person, not of some gaseous "immortal soul," but of the real person.

There are thousands of ways to imagine what this can mean, and most of them can serve as a comfort to the dying or to mourners just as it can mean a stimulus to the imagination. Those who have "modern" views of the physical body no doubt look at it differently than did those of long ago. Still, it is hard to imagine mourners of a thousand years ago who have seen their loved one burned to a cinder, or of a few wartime months ago who know their loved one has been blown to disintegrating bits, picturing that God scrapes up the atoms and molecules and sculpts a replica, breathing life into it. What Christian belief in the resurrection involves is contentment with mystery—the apostle Paul calls it that—and readiness for the riddle. What matters is confidence that after this life nothing "will be able to separate us from the love of God in Christ" (Romans 8:39) and that we are never removed from God's care. The Old Testament says little about this; one or two poetic passages open the conversation. The New Testament has varying views, all of them designed to bring comfort and none of them interested in providing flat scientific answers. Sometimes someone like Paul can speak of a "spiritual body," and that communicates something. No one speaks of the resurrection as the working of an "immortal soul," since the Bible says that immortality belongs alone to God.

It is natural at a time of loss and mourning to picture God's saints as having less of an existence than they did when their bodies were healthy. Whatever else the belief in the new creation means, it means not less but more, and that more is always a being-wrapped in the arms of divine love and presence.

82. What Is the Kingdom of God?

New Testament scholars have spilled much ink and made use of whole forests of wood-turned-to-paper to spell out in books what Jesus meant when he proclaimed the nearness of the kingdom of God. There is no reason for Christians to slap Christians who equate "kingdom" and "church," since they are pointing in the right direction. But technically they are wrong; Jesus does not equate the two and rarely is quoted talking about the church. For him, it is always the kingdom. The kingdom is not the church, in Lutheran teaching, but the church presupposes the kingdom. This means that as the believer sorts through what is going on when the Gospels or the New Testament letters invoke the kingdom, at least it refers to—borrowing the condensation of some scholars—"the sovereign, saving activity of God in Christ." The kingdom is not a spot on the map, but an activity; it can be a realm, but not a geographical place. In that realm the word and works of God are swirling and generating. It is "sovereign," meaning that it is entirely the work of God, who originates and sustains it and then invites the repentant into it, as Jesus did. It is "saving" activity, in that it always seeks to effect change and never leaves those who are swept up in it where they were. And it focuses "in Christ."

Jesus did not say that the kingdom of God is "within you," as some translation had it, but that it is "in your midst." He was pointing to himself. Where he was proclaiming good news, healing, calling for repentance, effecting justice, doing the words of love—*there* was the activity he called the kingdom. He also summoned his followers to announce the kingdom and to be part of its activity, so it still goes on. And since it is the "kingdom of God," there cannot be limits unless God is limited. The little church on the corner, the classroom where the kingdom language is studied, is not the kingdom. It is a result of the kingdom and it helps serve the kingdom. The kingdom is ahead of us, and it is here. God rules in both and all times and all places.

All Christian traditions wrestle with language not to do justice to the kingdom, but to point to it. For Lutherans, the Small Catechism points well in the language explaining the line in the Lord's Prayer, "Your kingdom come": "God's kingdom comes indeed without our praying for it, but we ask in this prayer that it may also come to us." The child or the learner then asks, "How does this come about?" One way to think about it is this: "Whenever our heavenly Father gives us his Holy Spirit, so that through the Holy Spirit's grace we believe God's Holy Word and live godly lives, here in time and hereafter in eternity."

Some of our contemporaries have the irritating habit of saying, "Whatever," when they want to step back and let anything happen or be included. Or if it is uncertain where people are to meet or where to establish something, the lazy person can shrug with a "wherever." In kingdom language nothing is going on as a "stepping back" or a lazy shrug. Ask about the kingdom and one can say, with a sweep of the hand, the scanning of an eye, and the reach of a tongue, "If God in Christ is present, then the kingdom is 'whatever,' and since it belongs everywhere, in the past, present, and future, 'hereafter in eternity,' it is fitting to say 'wherever.'" And mean it.

chapter thirteen

Polity

83. What Are the Main Features of the Lutheran Form of Church Government?

To talk about how to run the churchly show is a steep comedown from the glorious language we have just enjoyed about eternity, the resurrection, the kingdom of God, and blessedness. Consider it a kind of postscript, something one has to talk about even in an anti-climax, for the good reason that to advance the work described in the previous twelve chapters there cannot be simple or, for that matter, complicated chaos. Somehow congregations, confessions, denominations, federations, councils, and all the rest have to establish some sort of order. There are church bodies that make a great deal of this, as their very names show: Congregational, Presbyterian, Episcopal. Lutherans are stuck with the name of a human being who did not want the evangelical congregations to be labeled with his name. The fact that they settled for the name their enemies gave them shows that they were less preoccupied with the forms of church governments than many others. Still, they deal with the issue.

Sometimes Lutherans quote the comic of the 1930s, Will Rogers, who said, "I am not a member of any organized political party. I am a Democrat." So they might say, "I am not a member of the organized church. I am a Lutheran." That seems strange, given the ethnic background of so many tidy Lutherans in America: Scandinavian, German, Central European. These are people sometimes admired and sometimes resented for being obsessed with order, with having things lined up. In matters of church order, it is not that Lutherans *intended* to be disorderly. They simply had so many inheritances, so many influences, so many migrations, that they picked up features of many polities, or systems of government.

Thus one Lutheran body in the United States, the Evangelical Lutheran Church in America, chooses to be—it would say it is "called" to be—in full communion with bodies whose polities are describable as congregational, presbyterial, episcopal, synodical, conferential, and to these might soon be added another, connectional. Critics may say that such a mix is a sign of sloppiness, but Lutherans of this outlook would say that they are given to Christian freedom in such matters, and they are allowed to be pragmatists and to do what works, so long as they can affirm that they believe they were serious about the ties being God-pleasing in their intentions. Others may say that this is another expression of Lutherans that church polity is an "adiaphoron" (a matter of indifference), in some ways "neither here nor there."

To review: when Lutherans became Lutheran in Sweden as their king turned to Luther's version of the gospel, their bishops, in ties to the Church of England, kept those ties, and Swedish bishops were seen in continuity with the bishops, overseers, from the earliest Christian centuries. In some European places Lutherans rebelled against corrupt or lazy establishment bishops and turned congregational, like the Baptists and Congregationalists, acknowledging no higher authority than that of the local assembly. Often they borrowed from the way secular rulers governed. Now and then you will hear Lutherans say that if the church today would go "back to Luther," all would be well. On this topic one cannot go back to Luther and, if informed about the decisions made back then, should or would not want to. Luther and his colleagues inherited an episcopal system, but there were some problems. First, the bishops of the time were Roman Catholic, and they would not ordain the evangelicals who were coming to be called Lutheran. Second, bishops in that system were agents of the Holy Roman Empire, a government Lutherans were fighting. Those who want to romanticize Luther and think "back to Luther" as a way of settling polity issues are reluctant to do what practical church leader Luther did: he turned to the princes and had them be the authorizers of the ordaining of pastors, the prince being, in the language of the day, the "chief" believer or member. In our time doing something like this would mean turning to a governor to rule in churchly matters. Meanwhile, Luther and his peers spiritualized the governmental system by taking things into their own hands and doing the ordaining.

Today Lutherans in America tend to mix two ideas. First, with Luther, they like to think of the church as he did, as a gathering, a *Gemeinde* (a congregation), and thus ordinarily the most up-close, felt, and manageable expression. Yet those who have a vision of the kingdom and the church beyond the range of their own church steeple, and who recognize the need for allies and connections in the Body of Christ, or the empowerment that comes when one is not alone, do some connecting, via synods or other jurisdictions. These have various powers, seen as sanctioned but not determined by the Scriptures. What is decisive in Lutheran understanding is that the divine Word is properly preached and the sacraments rightly administered. Beyond that, most Lutherans believe they are free to work out various arrangements, and no one can read Lutheran history in America without seeing Lutherans constantly adapting, adjusting, improvising, within just a few boundaries.

84. What Is Ordination?

Whoever reads the reports of Lutheran bodies, or reads editorials about their actions, will find more debates about who is to be ordained and how they are to be ordained than about what ordination itself is. Lutherans in the century just past and in the new century have argued about the ordination of women or of homosexuals or of "unauthorized" candidates who have not "been through the process," without really settling on precisely what ordination means. Maybe they do not have to, and maybe they never will come to a conclusion on this matter. And if you imagine that I think I can solve the "who" issues in these few pages—or in many more!—for the varieties of Lutherans in America, be assured that I do not think so.

Having said that, it is important to note that, whatever it is, Lutherans *do* take ordination very seriously. They do want to be faithful to New Testament descriptions of what faithfulness in ministry would mean, and if ordination helps assure this, they celebrate it. They emphatically do not believe that the ordination of a person to the office of ministry, for the expression of the profession of ministry, lifts that person "above" those who exercise the ministry of the baptized. The ordained person is "set aside," not "placed above" in honor or status. The Lutheran Confessions say that a minister should be rightly called (*rite vocatus*), which does not give much of a clue or prescription. Lutheran churches insist on thorough theological, ministerial, and practical preparation. They may insist that the ordained be called to some form of congregational ministry, even if most of the exercise of ministry eventually is to be in seminary classrooms or agencies or chaplaincies. This is to honor the congregational base and to be sure that there is a hands-on context and that ministry is not remote or ethereal.

The origin of ordination is vague. Roman Catholics do not ordain women because, among other reasons, none are reported as having been present at the last supper, when they think that ordination first occurred. Lutherans do not follow this concept. They do observe ordination-like activities, for example in Acts 6:6 and 8:18, where those already in a ministry practiced "laying on of hands," still a sign or symbol, not a sacramental gesture in Lutheran ordinations. There is a strong recognition that the Holy Spirit is the agent of empowerment to this office. Ordination occurs in the presence of a congregation and is not a secret backdoor elevating. Yet the whole church is at least symbolically conceived of as being present. Ordination is not "indelible" and does not change the makeup of the ordinand. But it is expected that this person take very seriously the charge of the *whole* church under the Holy Spirit.

85. What Are Elders, and What Do They Do?

I mention elders because they are among the cast of characters in New Testament portrayals of administration in the earliest churches. Some bodies make much of their role. This is the case in the Presbyterian tradition, since the Greek word *presbyter* simply means "elder." Without taking the term into the denominational title, Lutherans take this elected office, under whatever name is favored, as a crucial expression of "the ministry of the baptized." The book of Acts and other writings show that elders were seen to have special competencies, gifts, and a readiness to engage in service and oversight. Various congregations assign varying tasks to elders. In the New Testament it was evidently assumed that the "elders" had experiences that the young did not have. They could provide vision, perspective, judgment, and balance. Today some twenty-five-year-olds show that you don't have to be elderly to be an elder. You have to be responsible, a student of Scripture, a diplomat, someone ready to admonish and be admonished, and a servant of the Word.

86. What Are Deacons, and What Do They Do?

Having shown how much freedom Lutherans have in naming offices and describing what goes on in them, it is hard not to step back and be precise and specific about the duties of different offices. In fact, many Lutherans may not even call those who fulfill diaconal roles "deacons." Every gathering of Christians, however, does need people to perform functions that the New Testament and Christians through the ages have associated with deacons. Sometimes they are called "board members" or "vestrymen" and "vestrywomen," and they may be associated with "trustees."

The Greek word *diakonia* means service of others, and deacons were to lead in that. All the baptized should engage in works of mercy, but it has been said that what is everybody's job is nobody's job, and deacons are representatives of certain tasks for the whole body and are to involve and inspire others. The early Christian communities attracted widows, the poor, and the helpless. There were no relief agencies and there was no Social Security. Those gathered by the Holy Spirit in Christ's name had to, or got to, do the work of ministering to them. Hence, deacons.

87. What Is a Synod, and What Does It Do?

Different church bodies have different terms for jurisdictions beyond the local level. Some call them "districts," and those who stress the place of bishops speak of "dioceses." We cannot get precise here. Rather, the accent now falls on the clustering of congregations within a specific region, which symbolizes the whole church or at least the whole confessional body, but which allows for reach beyond the merely local without losing the value of the local or the region. Synods are headed by a variety of officers in Lutheranism—bishops or presidents—who are surrounded by people with various competencies, talents, and assignments. They coordinate the work of congregations and usually carry out the supervising, credentialing, and authorizing of candidates for the ministry and other offices. They may propose candidates for ministry to congregations. They often offer the first line of arbitrators when there are irreconcilable conflicts in a local congregation, and they may be called upon to exercise discipline when it breaks down in the local church. And they get to provide counsel and aid, often in the form of subsidies or emergency funds, to help struggling congregations.

88. What Is Church Discipline, and Why Is It Important?

Church discipline is a biblically envisioned instrument to help ensure the integrity of a Christian body. The Gospels picture people within a gathering sometimes living in such a way that they offend or scandalize others, and then follow up with elaborate policies of how to deal with this—policies that give us a glimpse of how the first Christians did their disciplining. When Christianity was young and living in danger, it was especially important to know who belonged and was committed to the faith and the company. Those who led lives that brought disdain on the church weakened it. And Christians were often enough urged to tend to matters of doctrine and practice alike.

Constitutions of congregations and certainly of larger jurisdictions today spell out when to discipline, on what grounds, toward what intent. These are usually designed to protect the rights of the accused when there is controversy or misbehavior, but also they are to provide means of trying to right wrong, quicken consciences, and even, if tragically necessary, to follow biblical example by ruling someone out—with the hope that he or she, with a change of heart, will return.

Church discipline in our time often focuses on and even is restricted to the treatment of behavior and expression among ordained and other professional leaders. When sexual, behavioral, or fiscal issues are at stake, these not only affect the larger church body, but also often produce victims or breed scorn in the larger community. So the responsible leaders are called upon to exert influence and come to a decision, always with the good of the larger body and the accused in mind.

That may be a "downer" of an end to a book on Lutheran life, which, as suggested here, possesses vitalities and promise that the topic of church discipline can hardly express. Yet undisciplined church life, which is an offense against the gospel, is to be dealt with, says Lutheran teaching, so that the glories of the gospel are not dulled or compromised and so that the joy of Christian life, Lutheran style, lives on and reaches new people in a new millennium.

For Further Reading

Braaten, Carl E. *Principles of Lutheran Theology*, 2nd ed. Philadelphia: Fortress Press, 2007.

Daubert, Dave. *Living Lutheran: Reclaiming the "L" Word in Your Congregation*. Lutheran Voices. Minneapolis: Augsburg Fortress, 2007.

Evangelical Lutheran Worship. Minneapolis: Augsburg Fortress, 2006. Includes Small Catechism of Martin Luther.

Gritsch, Eric W. *Fortress Introduction to Lutheranism*. Minneapolis: Fortress Press, 1995.

Hinkle, Mary E. *Signs of Belonging: Luther's Marks of the Church and the Christian Life*. Lutheran Voices. Minneapolis: Augsburg Fortress, 2003.

Kolb, Robert, and Timothy J. Wengert, editors. *The Book of Concord: The Confessions of the Evangelical Lutheran Church*. Minneapolis: Fortress Press, 2000.

Lull, Timothy F. *On Being Lutheran: Reflections on Church, Theology, and Faith*. Foreword by Mark S. Hanson. Lutheran Voices. Minneapolis: Augsburg Fortress, 2006.

Lull, Timothy F., and William R. Russell, editors. *Martin Luther's Basic Theological Writings*, 2nd ed. Minneapolis: Fortress Press, 2005.

Marty, Martin. *Martin Luther*. New York: Penguin, 2004.

Skrade, Kristofer, and James Satter, editors. *The Lutheran Handbook*. Minneapolis: Augsburg Fortress, 2005.

Index of Topics

Made in the USA
San Bernardino, CA
08 July 2013